BACKPACK BOOKS

1,001 FACTS ABOUT

ROCKS AND MINERALS

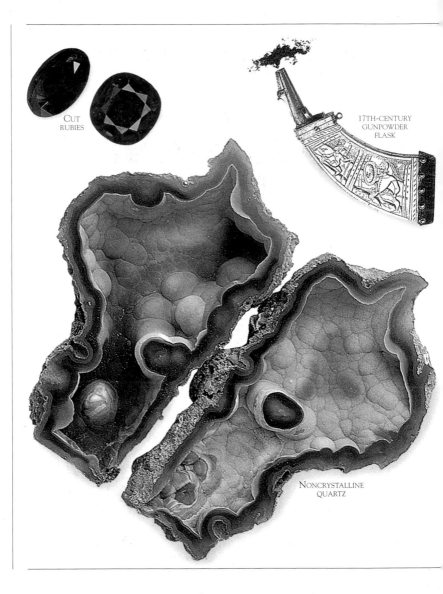

CUT
RUBIES

17TH-CENTURY
GUNPOWDER
FLASK

NONCRYSTALLINE
QUARTZ

BACKPACK BOOKS

1,001 FACTS ABOUT
ROCKS AND MINERALS

Written by SUE FULLER
With additional material by CHRIS MAYNARD

GNEISS

WATCH
WITH BRASS
CASE

CHALCOPYRITE

A Dorling Kindersley Book

LONDON, NEW YORK, MUNICH,
MELBOURNE, and DELHI

Project editor Clare Lister
Senior designer Adrienne Hutchinson
Senior editorial coordinator Camilla Hallinan
Senior design coordinator Sophia M Tampakopoulos Turner
DTP Jill Bunyan
Category publisher Sue Grabham
Production Linda Dare
With thanks to the original team:
Project editor Neil Bridges
Art editor Diane Clouting
Senior editor Susan McKeever
Senior art editor Helen Senior
Designer Alexandra Brown
Picture research Caroline Brooke
Production Louise Barratt

First American Edition, 2003
10 9 8 7 6

Published in the United States by
DK Publishing, Inc., 375 Hudson Street
New York, New York 10014

A catalog record for this book is available from the Library of Congress.

ISBN-13: 978-0-7894-9043-8

Color reproduction by Colourscan
Printed and bound in Singapore by Star Standard

See our complete product line at
www.dk.com

CONTENTS

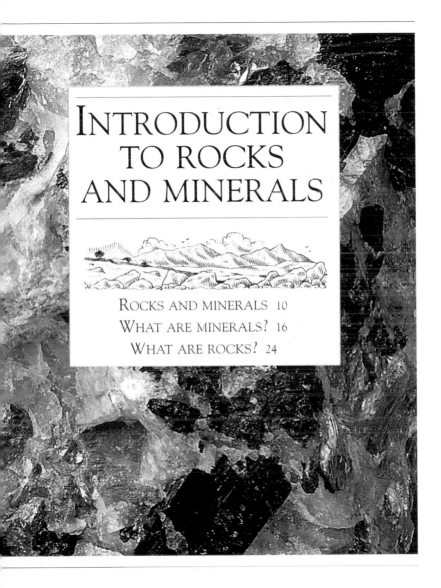

INTRODUCTION TO ROCKS AND MINERALS

9

ROCKS AND MINERALS

MINERALS ARE SOLID mixtures of chemicals that each have a set of characteristics – just like a fingerprint. Groups of minerals bind together in various ways to form rocks. The Earth's crust (surface layer) consists of these rocks. Below, you can see a rock called granite and the minerals that make it up.

Mica

COARSE-GRAINED GRANITE

Quartz

QUARTZ
The most common mineral in the Earth's crust is quartz. It forms the gray matrix (mass of rock in which other crystals are set) in the granite specimen.

Feldspar

FELDSPAR
Another common mineral that often forms part of rocks is feldspar. The white crystals shown here are a variety of feldspar called microcline. In the granite specimen, the feldspar crystals have a pinkish color.

MICA

The third mineral that typically occurs in granites, including the specimen shown, is mica. It also forms part of many other rocks. Biotite, shown below, is a black, platelike mica that is soft enough to scratch with a fingernail.

Tourmaline

A vein of white quartz and gold chalcopyrite cuts through this granite block

MINERAL VEIN IN GRANITE

Rocks can contain veins of precious minerals. The gold areas in this granite block are chalcopyrite, an ore of copper. An ore is a material from which metals are extracted.

CUT TOURMALINE

Precious gem minerals can also grow in rocks, especially in coarse-grained igneous rocks like granite. The large black crystals in the granite specimen and the cut gem shown here both consist of the mineral tourmaline.

PURPLE
TOURMALINE
GEMSTONE

GRANITE QUARRY

Rocks are quarried and mined for the minerals that make them up and the ores and gems they contain. They are also valuable themselves, for building and as aggregate (broken stone) for roads and railways. This granite quarry is near Slyudyanka, Russian Federation.

The Earth

Our planet is like an onion – it is made up of a number of layers. At the Earth's center, there is a metallic core. The next layer is the mantle. It consists of solid rock that flows slowly in huge currents. We live on the crust, the thin outer layer with its familiar continents and oceans.

MOVING PLATES

The Earth's crust is broken up into nine "panels" called plates. At the edges of the plates, new oceanic crust forms and is destroyed. This causes the plates to "float" around in the crust. The continents, such as Africa, form part of the plates and they move with them.

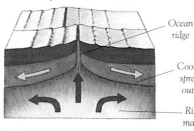

Ocean ridge

Cool rocks spreading outward

Rising magma

EURASIAN PLATE

AFRICAN PLATE

AFRICAN PLATE

ANTARCTIC PLATE

SPREADING OCEAN FLOOR

Oceanic crust forms at ocean ridges where magma (molten rock beneath the Earth's surface) rises and forms rock. As more magma follows, rocks are pushed sideways and the ocean floor spreads.

PLATE EDGES

The thin blue line toward the bottom of the diagram shows where the edges of the African and Antarctic plates meet.

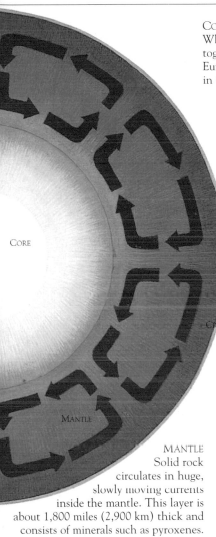

COLLIDING CONTINENTS
When two continents collide, they crunch together to form mountain ranges. The European Alps and the Himalayas formed in this way.

Mountains forming

Moving plate

Magma flow in mantle

AFRICAN AND EURASIAN PLATES
The blue line separating Africa and Europe on the diagram shows where the African and Eurasian plates have collided, bringing the two large continents together.

CRUST
The crust is a thin skin, only 43½ miles (70 km) deep at its thickest part. Beneath the oceans, the crust is much thinner, rarely more than 4½ miles (7 km) deep. The crust is cold and solid. It consists of continents and oceans.

CORE
A mixture of nickel and iron makes up the Earth's core. The inner core is solid and is about 850 miles (1,370 km) across. The outer core is wider, about 1,240 miles (2,000 km) deep. It is molten and moves. Movements in the outer core create the Earth's magnetic fields.

CORE

CRUST

MANTLE
Solid rock circulates in huge, slowly moving currents inside the mantle. This layer is about 1,800 miles (2,900 km) thick and consists of minerals such as pyroxenes.

13

The age of rocks and minerals

Rocks and minerals have formed since the beginning of time, and are still forming today. Written in these solid materials is a full history of the Earth. By studying rocks and minerals, scientists have calculated the age of the Earth and found out about the great events that have shaped our planet.

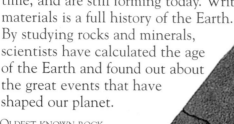

Chondrite is made up of small, crystalline grains

OLDEST KNOWN ROCK
The oldest known rocks come from outer space. This chondrite specimen, for example, is about 4,600 million years old. Although the Earth formed at about the same date, the first rocks didn't develop on our planet until later – about 4,200 million years ago.

ROCKS FORMING TODAY
New rocks are forming all the time, at the Earth's surface and in the crust below. This photograph taken from space shows the Nile delta in Egypt. When the Nile reaches the Mediterranean Sea, the sediment carried by the river settles on the sea floor. Over time, layers of sediment will form new rock. This rock will provide a permanent record of the environmental conditions of the 20th century.

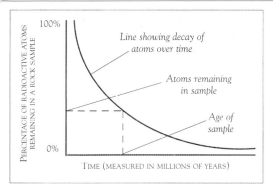

PERCENTAGE OF RADIOACTIVE ATOMS REMAINING IN A ROCK SAMPLE

100%

0%

Line showing decay of atoms over time

Atoms remaining in sample

Age of sample

TIME (MEASURED IN MILLIONS OF YEARS)

RADIOMETRIC DATING
Scientists have discovered a precise way of telling the age of rocks. It is called radiometric dating. Some radioactive atoms in rocks decay over time. By measuring the amount of these atoms remaining in a rock, scientists can calculate the age of the rock. This graph shows how to read this "geological clock."

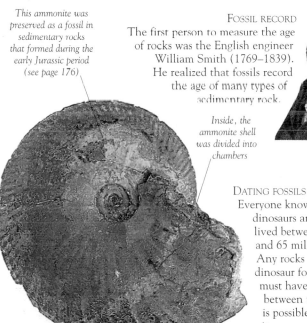

This ammonite was preserved as a fossil in sedimentary rocks that formed during the early Jurassic period (see page 176)

FOSSIL RECORD
The first person to measure the age of rocks was the English engineer William Smith (1769–1839). He realized that fossils record the age of many types of sedimentary rock.

Inside, the ammonite shell was divided into chambers

WILLIAM SMITH

AMMONITE FOSSIL

DATING FOSSILS
Everyone knows that the dinosaurs are extinct. They lived between about 245 and 65 million years ago. Any rocks that contain dinosaur fossils, therefore, must have formed between those dates. It is possible to date rocks quite accurately by studying the fossils they contain.

15

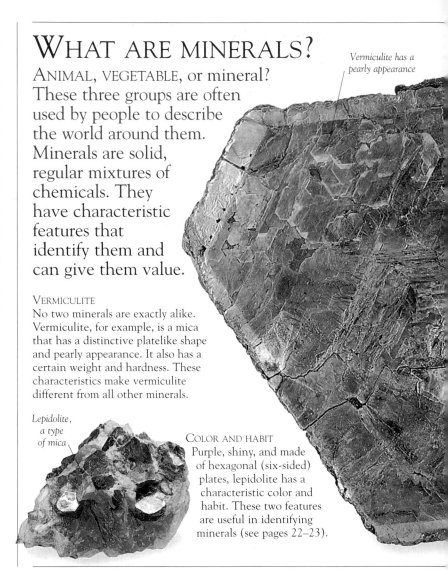

WHAT ARE MINERALS?

ANIMAL, VEGETABLE, or mineral?
These three groups are often
used by people to describe
the world around them.
Minerals are solid,
regular mixtures of
chemicals. They
have characteristic
features that
identify them and
can give them value.

*Vermiculite has a
pearly appearance*

VERMICULITE
No two minerals are exactly alike.
Vermiculite, for example, is a mica
that has a distinctive platelike shape
and pearly appearance. It also has a
certain weight and hardness. These
characteristics make vermiculite
different from all other minerals.

*Lepidolite,
a type
of mica*

COLOR AND HABIT
Purple, shiny, and made
of hexagonal (six-sided)
plates, lepidolite has a
characteristic color and
habit. These two features
are useful in identifying
minerals (see pages 22–23).

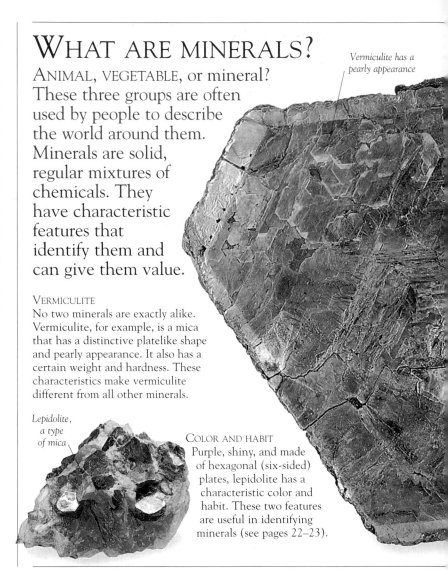

Distinctive platelike crystals

This model shows the atomic pattern of a mineral that is made up of thin sheets

PATTERN OF ATOMS
The elements that make up a mineral build it in a rigid atomic pattern that is always the same. The atoms may form flat, loosely linked sheets or in tight spheres. Each pattern gives different properties to a mineral, such as color, shape, hardness, weight, and cleavage.

Thin sheets of mica

CLEAVAGE
Many minerals break along lines of weakness called cleavage planes. This mica breaks into thin sheets. It consists of strongly bonded silicon and oxygen atoms, separated by weakly bonded atoms of iron, potassium, and magnesium.

Sheets separated by cleavage planes

ROCK-FORMING MINERALS
Minerals grow or cement together to form rocks. This mica pegmatite (a rock with large crystals) consists of three minerals – mica, quartz, and feldspar. These minerals formed rocks as magma cooled below the Earth's surface.

Large mica crystals

How minerals are formed

Minerals form in a huge range of environments – from human bones to the Earth's core. They grow from chemical ingredients called elements and may be affected by temperature and pressure as they develop. Some minerals, such as garnet, form over hundreds of thousands of years as heat and pressure gradually alter a rock. Olivine crystals, on the other hand, can grow several yards in an hour.

REALGAR
(ARSENIC ORE)

Bright red realgar crystals

HEMATITE
(IRON ORE)

GALENA
(LEAD ORE)

Metallic luster

MINERAL VEINS
Hot water circulates in many places in the Earth's crust – beneath volcanoes and hot springs, for example. This water carries a rich load of dissolved minerals – just like a chemical soup. The "soup" deposits minerals as it cools, forming mineral veins in cracks or cavities in rocks. These veins often contain valuable ores such as hematite, realgar, and galena.

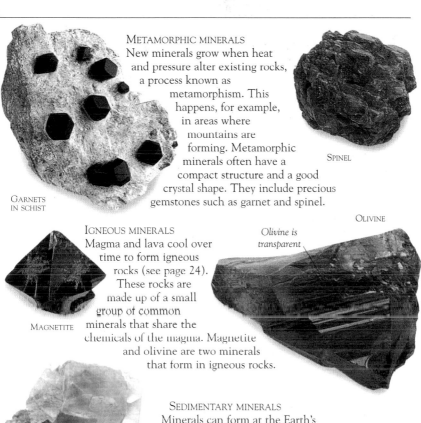

METAMORPHIC MINERALS
New minerals grow when heat and pressure alter existing rocks, a process known as metamorphism. This happens, for example, in areas where mountains are forming. Metamorphic minerals often have a compact structure and a good crystal shape. They include precious gemstones such as garnet and spinel.

GARNETS
IN SCHIST

SPINEL

OLIVINE

IGNEOUS MINERALS
Magma and lava cool over time to form igneous rocks (see page 24). These rocks are made up of a small group of common minerals that share the chemicals of the magma. Magnetite and olivine are two minerals that form in igneous rocks.

Olivine is transparent

MAGNETITE

SEDIMENTARY MINERALS
Minerals can form at the Earth's surface. Evaporating sea water, for example, leaves behind minerals like sylvite. Calcite, which forms limestone rock, also develops in sea water and in the skeletons of many living creatures.

White calcite crystals

CALCITE

SYLVITE

Identifying minerals

Minerals each possess a unique set of identifying properties. Six of the most important mineral properties are shown on the page opposite. To help you with identification, these six properties are featured in the fact boxes in the mineral section of this book. Minerals are also grouped into systems according to their crystal symmetry (regularity of form). The yellow symbols shown below represent the main crystal systems.

CUBIC
Minerals grouped in the cubic crystal system have the most regular symmetry. The fool's gold mineral pyrite is a good example.

MONOCLINIC
Gypsum belongs to the monoclinic system. This is one of the most common systems, but has less symmetry than the cubic system.

TRICLINIC
Crystals in the triclinic system have the least regular symmetry of the crystal systems. Rare axinite belongs to this system.

AXINITE

PYRITE

SELENITE
(VARIETY OF
GYPSUM)

TRIGONAL/
HEXAGONAL
These two similar systems are commonly grouped together as one. The precious mineral beryl falls into this system.

ORTHORHOMBIC
Minerals in this system develop crystals that have a symmetry similar to that of a matchbox. Barite is a member of this system.

TETRAGONAL
Idocrase is a mineral in the tetragonal system. Crystals have a set of long sides and square ends, a little like a stretched cube.

EMERALD
(VARIETY
OF BERYL)

BARITE

IDOCRASE

TALC

• SPECIFIC GRAVITY (SG)
You work out a mineral's specific gravity by comparing the weight of the mineral with the weight of an equal volume of water. Platinum has a specific gravity of 21.4.

PLATINUM

• HARDNESS
The hardness of a mineral is measured by how easily it scratches. Mohs' scale is the usual measure of mineral hardness. Talc is the softest mineral on the scale. It has a hardness of 1.

CINNABAR AND STREAK

• STREAK
If you crush a mineral into a powder, the color of the powder is known as streak. Cinnabar has a reddish-brown to scarlet streak.

AZURITE

• COLOR
Azurite can be identified by its blue color. Other minerals have many colors and must be identified in other ways.

BISMUTH

• TRANSPARENCY
A transparent mineral, such as celestine, allows light to pass through it. Opaque minerals do not allow any light to pass through them.

CELESTINE

• LUSTER
The way daylight reflects off the surface of a mineral is known as luster. This bismuth specimen has a shiny, metallic luster.

Mineral color and habit

The beauty of minerals comes from their color and habit (shape). Some minerals have more than one color. For example, red ruby and blue sapphire are both varieties of corundum. By contrast, yellow is the only color of sulfur and is useful in identifying this mineral. Habit can also be a guide to identification. Malachite, for instance, typically forms bubbly masses and crusts. Corundum tends to develop well-formed crystals.

UNCUT RUBIES AND SAPPHIRES

QUARTZ
Pure crystalline quartz is colorless. Colors appear when chemical impurities enter its crystal structure.

GYPSUM
Fibers of gypsum make up this specimen, which is pure in composition and colored white.

SILVER
Native silver often forms in a dendritic (branching) habit. Its characteristic color aids identification.

GOLD
Water-worn and rounded nuggets are one of the characteristic habits of valuable yellow gold.

SULFUR
This yellow mineral is idiochromatic – it gets its color because it only absorbs certain light rays.

TIGER'S EYE
This type of quartz has a silky appearance known as chatoyancy. Its colors resemble a tiger's eye.

RUBY
Tiny inclusions (other minerals enclosed in the crystal) give an attractive star effect in this red ruby.

TOURMALINE
This single crystal shows two of tourmaline's many colors, which are caused by chemical impurities.

MALACHITE
Only found in these green colors, malachite has a characteristic botryoidal (bubbly) habit.

TURQUOISE
This mineral always forms an encrusting or massive habit, which means it has no particular shape.

FLUORITE
Cubic crystal twins are a typical habit of fluorite. Twins are two crystals that are intergrown.

CLINOCLASE
Rare clinoclase grows in brilliant blue fibrous rosettes on the surface of other minerals.

HALITE
Errors in the atomic structure of this halite specimen color it blue. Pure halite is white.

LABRADORITE
This labradorite example shows iridescence, a play of colors on its surface like a film of oil on water.

HEMATITE
This hematite is also iridescent and shows the unusual crystalline variety of the mineral.

WHAT ARE ROCKS?

CRUMBLY PEAT AND hard-wearing granite may look and feel very different, but they are both rocks. Rocks are solid mixtures of minerals. Geologists classify rocks according to the way they are formed. The three main types are igneous, metamorphic, and sedimentary rocks.

GRANITE
(IGNEOUS ROCK)

Granite

IGNEOUS ROCK
Granite is an igneous rock. This rock type develops as molten magma and lava cool. The fragments of granite in the breccia formed deep underground in the Earth's crust.

BRECCIA
This rock specimen is known as breccia. It is a sedimentary rock made from existing fragments of all three major rock types. Geologists can discover the history of this rock by studying these fragments.

OOLITIC
LIMESTONE
(SEDIMENTARY
ROCK)

SEDIMENTARY ROCK
This rock is called oolitic limestone. It is a type of sedimentary rock that forms in sea water. Fragments of this type of limestone in the breccia indicate that the area in which the breccia formed was once covered by the sea. Sedimentary rocks record conditions at the Earth's surface.

Oolitic limestone

Folded gneiss

FOLDED GNEISS
(METAMORPHIC
ROCK)

METAMORPHIC ROCK
Gneiss is a metamorphic rock. It formed in conditions of great heat and pressure during mountain-building. Metamorphic rocks hold clues to processes that occur in the Earth's crust.

The rock cycle

Heat, pressure, weathering, and erosion are some of the processes by which the Earth recycles rocks. The elements and minerals that make up rocks are never destroyed, but used many times over.

IGNEOUS ROCKS FORM
Liquid magma (1) cools and solidifies to form igneous rocks. This may happen deep underground in intrusions, such as dykes (2), or at the Earth's surface.

WEATHERING AND EROSION
Movements in the Earth's crust bring rocks to the surface. Agents such as wind, water, and ice break up the rocks into particles. This is weathering. Glaciers (3) and rivers (5) carry the particles from their original site. This removal process is called erosion.

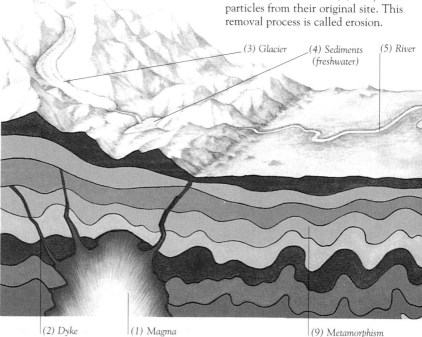

(3) Glacier *(4) Sediments (freshwater)* *(5) River*

(2) Dyke *(1) Magma* *(9) Metamorphism*

DEPOSITION AND METAMORPHISM

The rock particles may be deposited as sediments on land (6), in lakes (4), deltas (7), or farther out to sea (8). Strata, or layers of sediment, form as more material is deposited. The weight of successive layers of sediment compress and cement the particles. If the process stops there, sedimentary rocks are the result. Metamorphism (9) occurs if the rocks are deeply buried and heated. Heat and pressure transform old rocks and minerals into new.

ROCKS RECYCLED

Intense heat and pressure can melt rocks (11). This happens, for example, when two of the plates in the Earth's crust collide (10). Molten rocks may form new magma. Some magma returns to the Earth's surface through volcanoes (12). It erupts as lava (13) and hardens to form new igneous rock. Magma may also be recycled in the crust. When this magma cools, it forms in igneous intrusions, such as dykes, and the rock cycle begins once again.

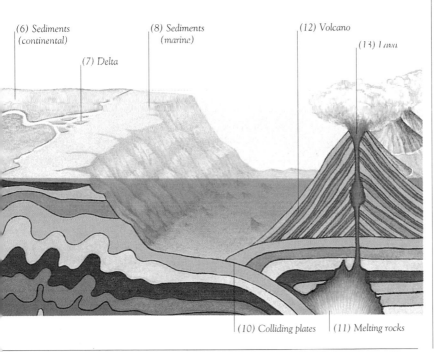

(6) Sediments
(continental)

(7) Delta

(8) Sediments
(marine)

(12) Volcano

(13) Lava

(10) Colliding plates

(11) Melting rocks

Identifying rocks

Rocks all have distinctive characteristics. You can often identify a rock specimen by making a few simple observations. All igneous and metamorphic rocks, for example, consist of interlocking crystals of different minerals. Crystals found in igneous rocks are usually randomly arranged. In metamorphic rocks, the crystals are often aligned into patterns, known as foliations. Sedimentary rocks are made of rock particles and minerals that are cemented together. On these pages, you can see some typical characteristics of igneous, metamorphic, and sedimentary rocks.

IGNEOUS ROCKS

GABBRO

BASALT

WHITE GRANITE

SLOW COOLING
Igneous rocks that form underground cool slowly. As a result, there is time for the rocks to develop large, well-formed crystals. Gabbro is an example of a slow-cooling igneous rock.

RAPID COOLING
Basalt is an example of an igneous rock that formed at the Earth's surface. It is similar to gabbro, but cools rapidly, and so consists of small, poorly developed crystals.

COLOR
Light-colored igneous rocks, such as this white granite, tend to be rich in silica. Dark-colored igneous rocks are usually silica-poor, but contain dark, heavy minerals.

METAMORPHIC ROCKS

SCHIST

SLATE WITH PYRITE

FOLDED GNEISS

FOLIATION
The action of pressure can align the crystals in metamorphic rocks. This gives rocks, such as this schist, a distinct foliated or wavy appearance.

PRESENCE OF MINERALS
Certain minerals grow in different conditions of heat and pressure. Pyrite often occurs in slate, for example. This rock forms in low heat and pressure.

SIZE OF CRYSTALS
Crystals grow slowly on metamorphic rocks. The large crystals in this gneiss indicate that it formed during long "cooking" in high heat and pressure.

SEDIMENTARY ROCKS

CONGLOMERATE

MILLET-SEED SANDSTONE

FRESHWATER LIMESTONE

PARTICLE SIZE
The size of particles in sedimentary rocks varies greatly – from the very coarse to the microscopic. Conglomerate is a rock that has coarse particles.

PARTICLE SHAPE
The shape of particles in sedimentary rocks shows how the particles have been transported. Desert winds rounded the particles in this sandstone.

PRESENCE OF FOSSILS
Fossils never occur in igneous rocks and only rarely in metamorphic rocks. They are common in many sedimentary rocks, such as this limestone.

MINERALS

DIAMOND

THE FIERY brilliance of diamond makes it the most valuable gemstone in the world. People have worn diamonds as jewelry for centuries. It is also used in industry because it is the hardest naturally occurring mineral. Drills and saws that have diamonds in their tips can cut through any other substance.

COLORED DIAMONDS

CUBIC

NATIVE DIAMOND
Diamonds, like this one from South Africa, are found in a rare type of volcanic rock called kimberlite. They also occur in river gravels, where they can easily be mistaken for worthless pebbles.

Rough diamond

Crown

DIAMOND FACTS
- Hardness: 10
- SG: 3.52
- Color: colorless or white; can be many other colors
- White streak
- Transparent to opaque
- Adamantine (bright) to greasy luster

CUTTING A DIAMOND
A skilled stone cutter and polisher, called a lapidary, starts with a rough stone. Looking at the stone through a powerful lens reveals the grain (planes of cleavage) and finds any flaws and impurities that cutting must mask.

1 GRINDING DOWN
The lapidary removes the top pyramid of the rough diamond and rounds the stone by grinding it against another diamond. This is known as bruting.

Cut diamonds sparkle in this silver brooch

DEEP FORMATION

Diamonds form in the Earth's mantle in conditions of extreme heat and pressure. At depths of about 93 miles (150 km), they develop a compact atomic structure that gives them their hardness. Volcanic eruptions bring the diamonds to the surface of the Earth.

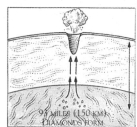

93 MILES (150 KM)
DIAMONDS FORM

GRADING
Diamonds are graded by four properties: cut, clarity, color, and carat. These are known as "the four Cs." A carat is a measure of weight.

A brilliant cut

Facets cut in sets of four

4 BRILLIANT FINISH
A finished cut diamond with 57 facets is called a brilliant. (Model diamonds are used in this cutting sequence.)

Table facet

3 ADDING FACETS
Sloping cuts add facets to the diamond in sets of four, to both the top and bottom of the stone.

2 DOPS AND TABLES
Cutting continues with the diamond fixed tightly to a stick called a dop. The lapidary cuts a flat table facet (one side of a cut gem) using an iron grinding wheel coated with diamond dust.

CUTTING TOOL
The hardness of diamond makes it a powerful industrial cutting tool and abrasive. Oil well drilling bits and surgeons' scalpels have diamonds in their tips.

DIAMOND
DRILL BIT

ROCK SALTS

HALITE AND SYLVITE belong to a range of minerals known as rock salts. These minerals form when salty water evaporates and dissolve again if placed in fresh water.

Orange halite crystals

CUBIC

NATIVE HALITE
Halite is known commonly as edible salt, and is identified by its taste. It occurs around modern seas and lakes in hot, dry climates. Halite is also found below ground in areas where these conditions existed in the past. Beneath the North Sea, there are layers of halite that formed about 260 million years ago.

SALTY SEA
One of the world's most salty seas is the Dead Sea in the Middle East, seen here in a 19th-century engraving. It has so much salt dissolved in it that people can float on its surface. Rock salts form around the water's edge.

HALITE FACTS

- Hardness: 2
- SG: 2.1–2.2
- Color: white, orange, red, purple, blue, black
- White streak
- Transparent to translucent
- Glassy luster

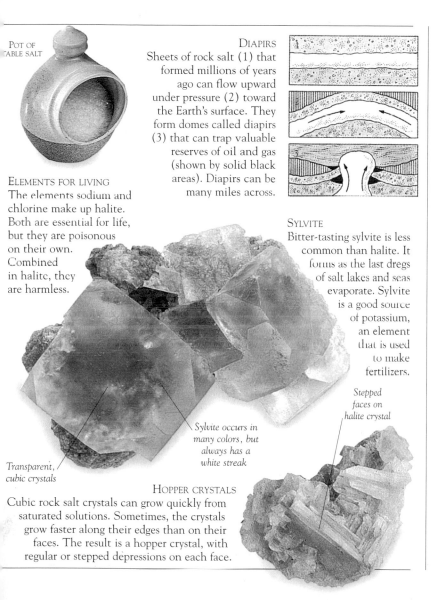

POT OF TABLE SALT

DIAPIRS
Sheets of rock salt (1) that formed millions of years ago can flow upward under pressure (2) toward the Earth's surface. They form domes called diapirs (3) that can trap valuable reserves of oil and gas (shown by solid black areas). Diapirs can be many miles across.

ELEMENTS FOR LIVING
The elements sodium and chlorine make up halite. Both are essential for life, but they are poisonous on their own. Combined in halite, they are harmless.

SYLVITE
Bitter-tasting sylvite is less common than halite. It forms as the last dregs of salt lakes and seas evaporate. Sylvite is a good source of potassium, an element that is used to make fertilizers.

Stepped faces on halite crystal

Sylvite occurs in many colors, but always has a white streak

Transparent, cubic crystals

HOPPER CRYSTALS
Cubic rock salt crystals can grow quickly from saturated solutions. Sometimes, the crystals grow faster along their edges than on their faces. The result is a hopper crystal, with regular or stepped depressions on each face.

CALCITE

A ROCK FORMING mineral, calcite is found in limestone and most seashells. This rock former is very common at the Earth's surface. It dissolves in water and grows anywhere that water can reach.

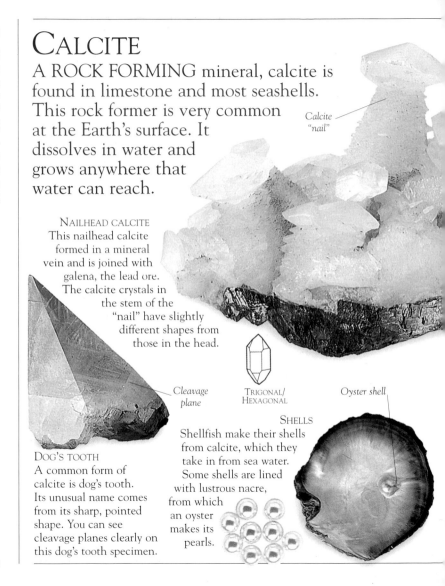

Calcite "nail"

NAILHEAD CALCITE
This nailhead calcite formed in a mineral vein and is joined with galena, the lead ore. The calcite crystals in the stem of the "nail" have slightly different shapes from those in the head.

Cleavage plane

TRIGONAL/ HEXAGONAL

Oyster shell

SHELLS
Shellfish make their shells from calcite, which they take in from sea water. Some shells are lined with lustrous nacre, from which an oyster makes its pearls.

DOG'S TOOTH
A common form of calcite is dog's tooth. Its unusual name comes from its sharp, pointed shape. You can see cleavage planes clearly on this dog's tooth specimen.

GROWING ROCK

Stalactites hang from the ceilings of limestone caves. They grow when calcite precipitates (forms thin deposits) from dripping water. In the warmth and low pressures of the caves, the water evaporates and leaves a small deposit of calcite. Stalagmites grow where the water drops to the floor.

Growth rings

Stalactites grow a few millimeters a year.

CALCITE TERRACES

The Pamukkale Falls, Turkey, formed as calcite precipitated from hot spring water. The mineral hardened to form a succession of terraces.

Galena

CALCITE FACTS

- Hardness: 3
- SG: 2.71
- Color: white or colorless, gray, red, brown, green, black
- White streak
- Transparent to translucent
- Glassy, pearly, or dull luster

SEEING DOUBLE

An image seen through calcite appears double. The name of this optical effect is double refraction.

Double refraction in transparent calcite

BARITE

IF YOU PICK UP a sample of barite, you will be surprised at how heavy it feels. This mineral weighs much more than its crystalline form suggests. In fact, it is heavier than some metallic minerals. Barite has many uses in industry and everyday life.

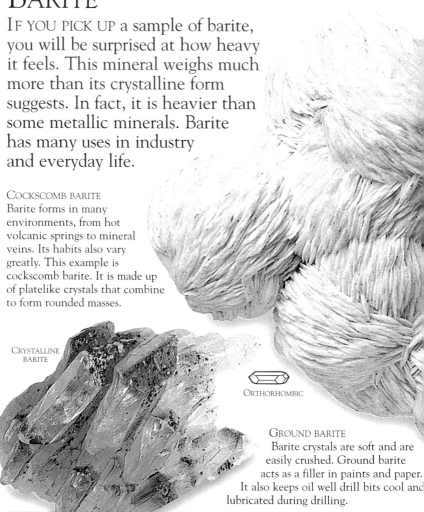

COCKSCOMB BARITE
Barite forms in many environments, from hot volcanic springs to mineral veins. Its habits also vary greatly. This example is cockscomb barite. It is made up of platelike crystals that combine to form rounded masses.

CRYSTALLINE BARITE

ORTHORHOMBIC

GROUND BARITE
Barite crystals are soft and are easily crushed. Ground barite acts as a filler in paints and paper. It also keeps oil well drill bits cool and lubricated during drilling.

Pearly luster on surfaces of tiny, platelike crystals

BARITE FACTS

- Hardness: 3–3.5
- SG: 4.5
- Color: colorless to white; can be many other colors
- White streak
- Transparent to translucent
- Glassy to pearly luster

DESERT ROSE
Any mineral collector would be happy to own this barite desert rose. It formed in a desert environment when water evaporated quickly in dry heat. Impurities in the water were left behind and formed crystals like petals.

Crystals that grew out from the center form "petals"

GYPSUM

SELENITE CRYSTAL

PLASTER OF PARIS, alabaster, fertilizers, and some types of explosive all contain gypsum. This mineral develops at the Earth's surface. It forms wherever water evaporates and in the mud around hot volcanic springs. Gypsum is an extremely common substance that is mined on a large scale in many parts of the world.

Crystals radiate from a central point

RADIATING CRYSTALS
Gypsum can form as fibers or needles that radiate from a central point. Known as daisy gypsum, this habit looks like petals on a flower. Several bunches of these "flowers" may grow in one gypsum bed.

Translucent gypsum twin

Crystal mass

DAISY GYPSUM

TWINNED CRYSTALS
Gypsum crystals often grow in twins. These are crystals of the same mineral that grow together, but in slightly different directions. Common types of gypsum twins are "fish-" or "swallow-tails," so called because of their forked shape. These crystals are from Winnipeg, Canada.

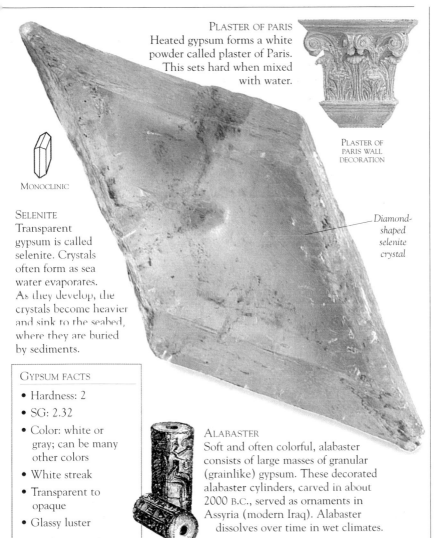

PLASTER OF PARIS
Heated gypsum forms a white powder called plaster of Paris. This sets hard when mixed with water.

PLASTER OF
PARIS WALL
DECORATION

MONOCLINIC

SELENITE
Transparent gypsum is called selenite. Crystals often form as sea water evaporates. As they develop, the crystals become heavier and sink to the seabed, where they are buried by sediments.

Diamond-shaped selenite crystal

GYPSUM FACTS

- Hardness: 2
- SG: 2.32
- Color: white or gray; can be many other colors
- White streak
- Transparent to opaque
- Glassy luster

ALABASTER
Soft and often colorful, alabaster consists of large masses of granular (grainlike) gypsum. These decorated alabaster cylinders, carved in about 2000 B.C., served as ornaments in Assyria (modern Iraq). Alabaster dissolves over time in wet climates.

41

BERYL

THE COLOR OF BERYL changes its name and value. The pure mineral is colorless, but green emerald and blue-green aquamarine are the best-known varieties. Beryl is rare and very hard. These qualities combine with its fine colors to make it a desirable gemstone.

PRISMATIC CRYSTALS
Beryl forms deep in the Earth's crust. It most commonly occurs in granites and pegmatites (rocks with large crystals). These beryl crystals are prismatic, which means they are longer in one direction than the other.

CUT BERYL
GEMSTONES

COLORS
Small amounts of impurities give beryl its many colors. For instance, chromium or vanadium colors emerald green. Manganese gives morganite (pink beryl) its color.

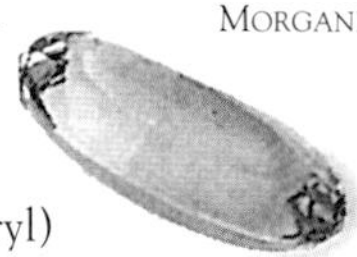

MORGANITE

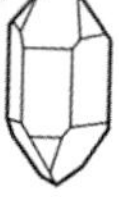

HELIODOR
Iron gives heliodor its rich yellow color. This rare variety of beryl derives its name from the Greek word for the Sun, *helios*.

TRIGONAL/
HEXAGONAL

Emerald in mass of calcite crystals

Prismatic beryl crystal

EMERALD
Green beryl is known as emerald. The finest examples of this precious stone come from Colombia, where they have been mined for centuries. Other sources are Pakistan, Zambia, and Zimbabwe. This prismatic emerald lies in a bed of calcite crystals.

COLOR OF THE SEA
Aquamarine is the color of sea water, and that is the literal meaning of its name. Iron gives this variety of beryl its color. Aquamarine is less valuable than emerald, but was popular for jewelry in the 19th century.

Color given by small amounts of iron

BERYL FACTS
- Hardness: 7–8
- SG: 2.6–2.9
- Color: colorless or white when pure; can be many other colors
- White streak
- Transparent to translucent
- Glassy luster

SPANISH EMERALDS
The Spanish introduced Colombian emeralds into Europe in the early 1500s. Many were treasures taken from the conquered native civilizations of Central and South America. This Spanish gold brooch dates from about 1650. It is set with 66 emeralds.

43

CRYSTALLINE QUARTZ

GOLDEN BEACH SAND and purple amethyst are both made of quartz. This mineral occurs in many rocks and is extremely common in the Earth's crust. Quartz crystals produce an electric charge if pressure is applied to them. This important property, known as piezoelectricity, gives quartz many uses and contributes to its value.

QUARTZ CRYSTALS
Crystals of quartz are common to most mineral collections. Typically, they have six sides and a top shaped like a pyramid. Quartz is a resistant mineral that represents hardness 7 on Mohs' scale. It is more hard-wearing than some gemstones.

TRIGONAL/
HEXAGONAL

CRYSTALLINE QUARTZ FACTS

- Hardness: 7
- SG: 2.65
- Color: colorless or white; can be many other colors
- White streak
- Transparent to translucent
- Glassy luster

MINERAL VEINS
Quartz often forms in mineral veins, such as these shown in a 19th-century engraving. Veins are cracks or faults in rocks into which hot, mineral-rich water flows. Quartz crystals develop as the water cools down.

Characteristic six-sided crystal with top shaped like a pyramid

AMETHYST
Purple quartz is called amethyst. Its color comes from tiny quantities of iron. Amethyst was very popular in 19th-century jewelry.

CITRINE
Slow heating turns amethyst into citrine, a yellow variety of quartz. Citrine rarely occurs in natural deposits and is a valuable collector's item.

DISCOVERY
The brothers Jacques and Pierre Curie discovered the property of piezoelectricity in quartz crystals.

RECORD PLAYER
Piezoelectric quartz crystals (hidden in a case in this picture) form part of a record player. They turn vibrations caused by the stylus running through record grooves into an electric charge. Speakers then convert the electric charge into sound that people can hear.

Case holding quartz crystals

Stylus

NONCRYSTALLINE QUARTZ

CHALCEDONY IS THE NAME given to most noncrystalline quartz. It describes agate, jasper, carnelian, and chrysoprase. Other varieties of noncrystalline quartz are flint and opal. All of these minerals develop in cracks or cavities in rocks that become filled with quartz-rich water.

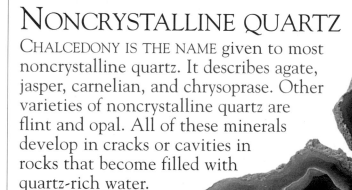

CHALCEDONY
Once split open, this rock from Brazil revealed an inner secret. Its core is made of chalcedony. A lining of agate surrounds the core. Chalcedony consists of tiny quartz fibers and can grow into almost any shape.

BLACK OPAL

TRIGONAL/ HEXAGONAL

SCATTERING LIGHT
Millions of tiny spheres of noncrystalline quartz make up opal. They reflect and scatter light to give a play of colors on the surface of the mineral.

OPAL MINES
The fine colors in opal make it a precious gemstone. Most opal comes from Australia, where it occurs in sedimentary rocks. These earth mounds are the result of opal mining at Coober Pedy, South Australia.

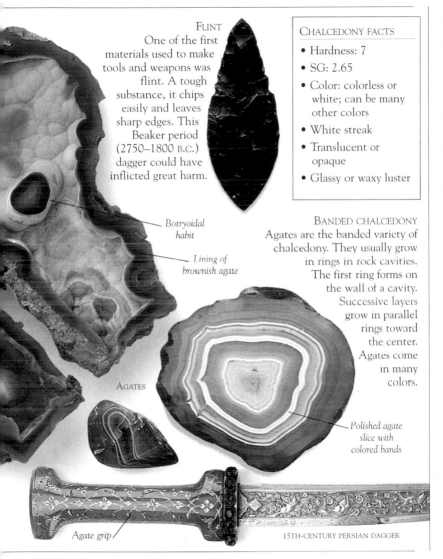

FLINT

One of the first materials used to make tools and weapons was flint. A tough substance, it chips easily and leaves sharp edges. This Beaker period (2750–1800 B.C.) dagger could have inflicted great harm.

Botryoidal habit

Lining of brownish agate

BANDED CHALCEDONY

Agates are the banded variety of chalcedony. They usually grow in rings in rock cavities. The first ring forms on the wall of a cavity. Successive layers grow in parallel rings toward the center. Agates come in many colors.

AGATES

Polished agate slice with colored bands

Agate grip

15TH-CENTURY PERSIAN DAGGER

FELDSPARS

A COMMON MINERAL group, feldspars form part of most types of rock, and occur in igneous, metamorphic, and sedimentary regions. Feldspar crystals vary greatly in size. Large examples can be up to 20 ft (6 m) long, while the smallest are microscopic. The uses of feldspars also vary – from fine jewelry to materials for building.

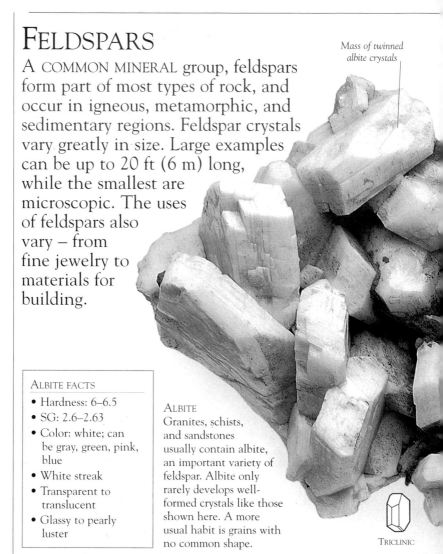

Mass of twinned albite crystals

ALBITE FACTS

- Hardness: 6–6.5
- SG: 2.6–2.63
- Color: white; can be gray, green, pink, blue
- White streak
- Transparent to translucent
- Glassy to pearly luster

ALBITE
Granites, schists, and sandstones usually contain albite, an important variety of feldspar. Albite only rarely develops well-formed crystals like those shown here. A more usual habit is grains with no common shape.

TRICLINIC

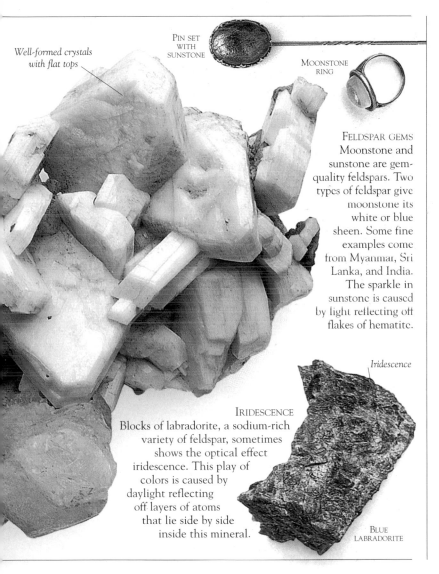

Well-formed crystals
with flat tops

PIN SET
WITH
SUNSTONE

MOONSTONE
RING

FELDSPAR GEMS
Moonstone and
sunstone are gem-
quality feldspars. Two
types of feldspar give
moonstone its
white or blue
sheen. Some fine
examples come
from Myanmar, Sri
Lanka, and India.
The sparkle in
sunstone is caused
by light reflecting off
flakes of hematite.

Iridescence

IRIDESCENCE
Blocks of labradorite, a sodium-rich
variety of feldspar, sometimes
shows the optical effect
iridescence. This play of
colors is caused by
daylight reflecting
off layers of atoms
that lie side by side
inside this mineral.

BLUE
LABRADORITE

MICAS

PICK A TYPICAL metamorphic or igneous rock and it is likely to contain a mica. Micas are a common group of rock-forming minerals that can develop very large crystals. They are made up of sheets of silica that readily part like the pages of a book.

Flaky muscovite from Minas Gerais, Brazil

MUSCOVITE FACTS

- Hardness: 2.5–4
- SG: 2.77–2.88
- Color: white to grayish; can be many other colors
- Colorless streak
- Transparent to translucent
- Glassy to pearly luster

MUSCOVITE
White mica is known as muscovite, a mineral that forms part of many igneous and metamorphic rocks. Muscovite crystals can be impressive. The largest measure up to 13 ft (4 m) across, and single crystals can weigh 2 tons.

MONOCLINIC

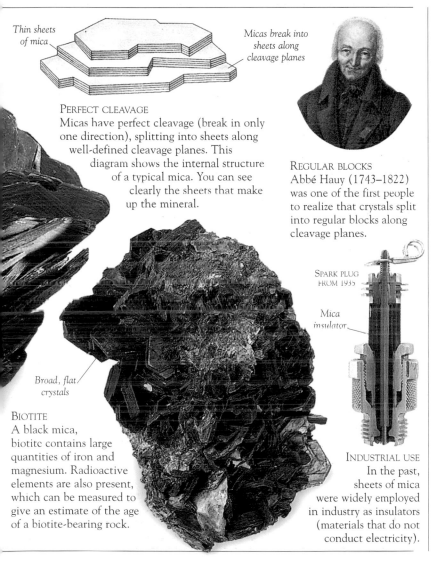

Thin sheets of mica

Micas break into sheets along cleavage planes

PERFECT CLEAVAGE

Micas have perfect cleavage (break in only one direction), splitting into sheets along well-defined cleavage planes. This diagram shows the internal structure of a typical mica. You can see clearly the sheets that make up the mineral.

REGULAR BLOCKS

Abbé Hauy (1743–1822) was one of the first people to realize that crystals split into regular blocks along cleavage planes.

SPARK PLUG FROM 1935

Mica insulator

BIOTITE

A black mica, biotite contains large quantities of iron and magnesium. Radioactive elements are also present, which can be measured to give an estimate of the age of a biotite-bearing rock.

Broad, flat crystals

INDUSTRIAL USE

In the past, sheets of mica were widely employed in industry as insulators (materials that do not conduct electricity).

COLORLESS AND WHITE

51

CORUNDUM

RUBIES AND SAPPHIRES are both rare and valuable forms of corundum. This mineral comes in many colors, but it is colorless when pure. Rating highly on Mohs' scale (9), corundum is very hard.

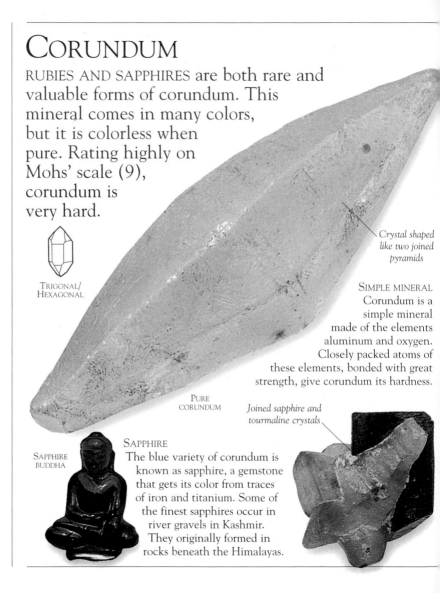

TRIGONAL/
HEXAGONAL

Crystal shaped like two joined pyramids

SIMPLE MINERAL
Corundum is a simple mineral made of the elements aluminum and oxygen. Closely packed atoms of these elements, bonded with great strength, give corundum its hardness.

PURE
CORUNDUM

Joined sapphire and tourmaline crystals

SAPPHIRE
BUDDHA

SAPPHIRE
The blue variety of corundum is known as sapphire, a gemstone that gets its color from traces of iron and titanium. Some of the finest sapphires occur in river gravels in Kashmir. They originally formed in rocks beneath the Himalayas.

HARD WORKER
The hardness of corundum makes it a useful mineral. Small grains are called emery, and are used in sandpaper. Many watches, such as this one, are set with rubies to protect their moving parts.

Rubies set in wristwatch

Flattened crystals are typical

CUT RUBIES

RUBIES
True red corundum is called ruby. Traces of chromium give this precious stone its color. The finest examples come from Myanmar, but Afghanistan and Pakistan are other sources. Rubies are most commonly found in river gravels.

Ruby from the Mogok region of Myanmar

HEALING RUBIES
Some people believe that rubies can help to prevent illness.

PEACOCK THRONE
Thousands of precious gems adorned the famous Peacock Throne of Shah Jahan, a 17th-century ruler of Persia (today's Iran). Among them were 108 rubies.

> CORUNDUM FACTS
> * Hardness: 9
> * SG: 4–4.1
> * Color: colorless when pure; can be many other colors
> * White streak
> * Transparent to translucent
> * Glassy luster

SILVER

BUNCHES OF WIRES and treelike branches are two common habits of silver. This metallic mineral can occur as a native element or mixed with other minerals. The main source of silver today is galena. Silver's value comes from its rarity and many uses. Jewelry and money were ancient uses of this metal. Today, it is also important in the photographic and electronics industries.

Shiny, treelike branches of silver

NATIVE SILVER
When silver occurs in its native form, it frequently develops as bunches of wires. Some of the finest examples of this habit of silver come from the area around Kongsberg, Norway.

DENDRITES
Another common habit of native silver is treelike branches. These are known as dendrites. You can clearly see the dendrites on this rock matrix from the Northern Territory, Australia.

BROWNIE CAMERA

CUBIC

PHOTOGRAPHY
The Brownie camera, launched in the 1900s, opened the photographic era. Today, photography is an industry that consumes most of the world's silver.

ORE CRUSHERS
Most of today's silver comes from ores such as galena. Crushing is the first stage in separating the mineral from its ore. These silver-ore crushers are at Taxco, Mexico.

Metallic luster

Decorative scratches

SILVER FACTS

- Hardness: 2.5–3
- SG: 10.5
- Color: silvery-white
- Shiny-gray streak
- Opaque
- Metallic luster

SILVER BEAKER
This silver "portrait beaker" is from South America. Silver is soft enough to be beaten into shape and can be scratched. It also bends rather than snaps. These qualities have made silver a popular metal for jewelry and ornaments for centuries.

PLATINUM

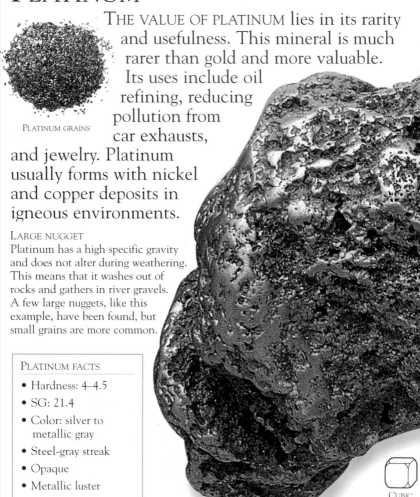

THE VALUE OF PLATINUM lies in its rarity and usefulness. This mineral is much rarer than gold and more valuable. Its uses include oil refining, reducing pollution from car exhausts, and jewelry. Platinum usually forms with nickel and copper deposits in igneous environments.

PLATINUM GRAINS

LARGE NUGGET
Platinum has a high specific gravity and does not alter during weathering. This means that it washes out of rocks and gathers in river gravels. A few large nuggets, like this example, have been found, but small grains are more common.

PLATINUM FACTS
- Hardness: 4–4.5
- SG: 21.4
- Color: silver to metallic gray
- Steel-gray streak
- Opaque
- Metallic luster

CUBIC

PLATINUM COINS
Like many precious metals, platinum has been used in coins. The Russians struck these platinum coins during the reign of Nicholas I in the 19th century.

Rugged surface

REDUCING POLLUTION
Catalytic converters reduce pollution from cars. These devices contain tiny amounts of platinum. The mineral helps turn poisonous fumes from the engine into less harmful gases.

Metallic luster

GRAPHITE

DIAMOND AND GRAPHITE are both made of pure carbon, but have very different properties. Diamond is the hardest mineral, while graphite is one of the softest. Graphite can be cut with a knife and marks paper, hence its use in pencils. The difference between the two minerals is in their internal structures.

MASSIVE GRAPHITE
Graphite usually has a massive habit or forms thin skins on the surface of other minerals. Crystals rarely form. Graphite is a native mineral that occurs in metamorphic rocks, including altered limestone, schists, and coal seams.

FISSION
Huge graphite rods form part of the reactor core of some nuclear power stations, such as this one under construction. Power is generated by nuclear fission. This is when uranium atoms in the reactor split at high speed and release energy. The graphite rods help control the speed of fission.

Carbon atoms in
bonded layers

GRAPHITE
PENCIL

DIAMONDS

LAYERS OF ATOMS
This model of graphite shows
strongly bonded layers of
carbon atoms separated by
weakly bonded layers. Graphite
is soft because the strong
layers slide over the weak.

Model of the internal
structure of diamond,
showing each atom
bonded to four others

STRUCTURE OF DIAMOND
Like graphite, diamond is made up of
carbon atoms. It is the way that these
atoms fasten together, however, that
gives diamond its hardness (10 on
Mohs' scale). Each carbon atom
in diamond bonds with four
others to give a rigid structure.

Shiny
surface

Graphite has a
characteristic
greasy feel

TRIGONAL/
HEXAGONAL

GRAPHITE FACTS

- Hardness: 1–2
- SG: 2.2
- Color: dark gray or
  black
- Gray-black streak
- Opaque
- Shiny, wet luster

GALENA

SINCE ROMAN TIMES, galena has been a valuable mineral, principally as the ore for lead and silver. Galena is a common mineral that solidifies in hydrothermal veins. These are cracks in rocks at higher levels in the Earth's crust that fill with hot, mineral-rich solutions.

CUBIC GALENA

CUBIC

CUBIC CRYSTALS
Galena usually develops cubic crystals and often forms twins. "Steps" are another common feature on broken crystal faces. This specimen clearly shows all these properties.

"*Steps*" *on broken crystal faces*

SILVERY-GRAY COLOR
The broken face of this example of galena reveals two features of this mineral. These are its dark silvery-gray color and its cubic crystal structure.

SPLIT GALENA

BLOCK CLEAVAGE
Galena crystals cleave into cubes or blocks along three well-defined planes of weakness, as shown in this simple diagram.

Large mass of twinned galena crystals with shiny, metallic luster

Carved silver plaque showing a hunting scene

CAT'S WHISKER RADIO
Some radio receivers in the 1920s used crystals of galena. The radios, such as the one above, picked up a signal when the operator moved a thin copper wire against a galena crystal. The wire was often known as a cat's whisker.

SILVER ORE
Galena is a silver ore. There are about 2.2 lb (1 kg) of the valuable metal in 1 ton of galena. Silver has been used to make precious objects since ancient times. This silver plaque dates from about 1600.

Lead strips (cames) in a 19th-century window

FLEXIBLE METAL
Another useful mineral extracted from galena is lead. This metal melts and bends easily, making it ideal for seals and pipes. In the past, lead was important in plumbing. Today, it is used for roofing and in windows.

GALENA FACTS

- Hardness: 2.5
- SG: 7.58
- Color: silvery-gray
- Dark gray streak
- Opaque
- Metallic luster

GOLD

FEW MINERALS have the importance and value of gold. This rare native element has been used since ancient times as a measure and store of wealth. Gold is a dense, heavy metal with a high specific gravity, but it is soft and easy to work. Jewelers sometimes mix gold with other metals, such as silver and copper, to make it harder.

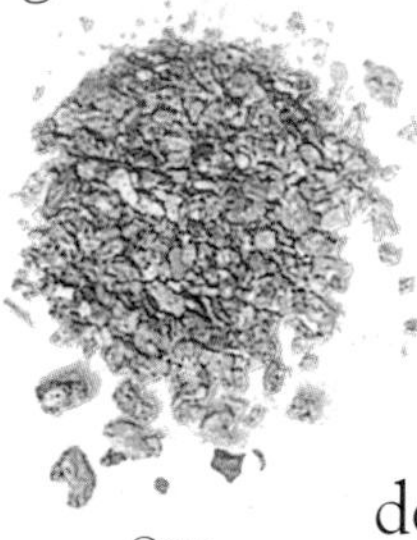

GOLD GRAINS

GOLD FACTS

- Hardness: 2.5–3
- SG: 19.3
- Color: bright yellow on fresh surfaces
- Golden-yellow streak
- Opaque
- Metallic luster

GOLD NUGGET
Few people will ever find a bright-colored gold nugget such as this example. Nuggets are extremely rare. They are usually crystalline and are often rounded at the edges due to weathering.

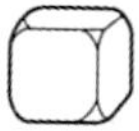

CUBIC

PANNING FOR GOLD
The prospect of finding gold started gold rushes in California and Australia in the 19th century. In this engraving, prospectors pan river gravels for the metal.

WORKING WITH GOLD
The Incas from Peru were skilled in working with gold. This scene shows two Inca goldsmiths making objects with a furnace and a mold.

Coiled monsters carved in gold

GOLD JEWELRY
This 14th-century English brooch is made of gold and decorated with gemstones. Gold is ideal for making jewelry because it is soft and easily worked into shape. This metal is also valued because it does not tarnish (lose its color or luster) in the open air.

Crystals with rounded edges

GROWING ON QUARTZ
Gold and quartz often grow together in mineral veins when hot, watery liquids cool. The gold sometimes forms a crust on the surface of the quartz crystals, as in this example. More usually, it is spread throughout the quartz. Smelting (heating) separates the two minerals.

Gold crystals form a crust on quartz

SULFUR

POWDERED SULFUR

THE NATIVE ELEMENT SULFUR is a surprising mineral. It is poisonous, yet is used as a medicine. It is bright yellow, but burns with a blue flame if held over a lighted match. Sulfur is also a valuable mineral that is mined on a large scale. It forms around hot springs and volcanic craters. Deposits also occur near diapirs below the Earth's surface.

SULFUR CRYSTALS
Crystals are a common form of sulfur. They are soft and can be easily cut with a knife. Pure crystals are always yellow, but impurities can color them brown or black.

ORTHORHOMBIC

Crust of sulfur crystals on volcanic rock from Java, Indonesia

SULFUR MINING
Heated brine (salty water) is used to mine layers of sulfur around salt diapirs. It is pumped below ground into the mineral deposit. The sulfur dissolves in the brine and flows back to the surface.

STEAM VENT
Sulfur crystallizes around volcanic vents and craters. There are clusters of crystals at the opening of this fumarole (steam vent). They formed when hot, sulfur-rich gases reached the cool open air.

Sulfur-rich gas

Flat-topped crystals with characteristic yellow color

This sample comes from Sicily, a major source of sulfur.

Black gunpowder

17TH-CENTURY GUNPOWDER FLASK

VOLCANIC CRATER
A carpet of sulfur covers a volcanic crater in Java. Inside the crater, a scientist wearing a mask collects samples of gas rich in sulfur. These samples can hold clues to the makeup of the rocks inside the volcano.

GUNPOWDER
The ancient Chinese discovered how to make gunpowder from sulfur. The mineral is still used in explosives today. Another important use is in vulcanization, which is when sulfur is added to rubber to make it stronger and more elastic.

SULFUR FACTS
- Hardness: 1.5–2.5
- SG: 2–2.5
- Color: yellow; impurities may give it other colors
- White streak
- Transparent to translucent
- Greasy luster

FOOL'S GOLD

GOLD IS RARE and precious. There is, however, a common group of minerals that can be mistaken for gold. Known as fool's gold, these minerals are also valuable and beautiful in their own right. Pyrite, for instance, replaces bones and shells in fossils, and chalcopyrite is a valuable ore.

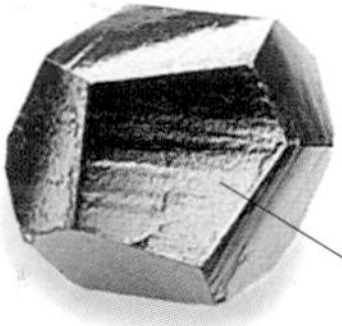

Crystal face with five sides

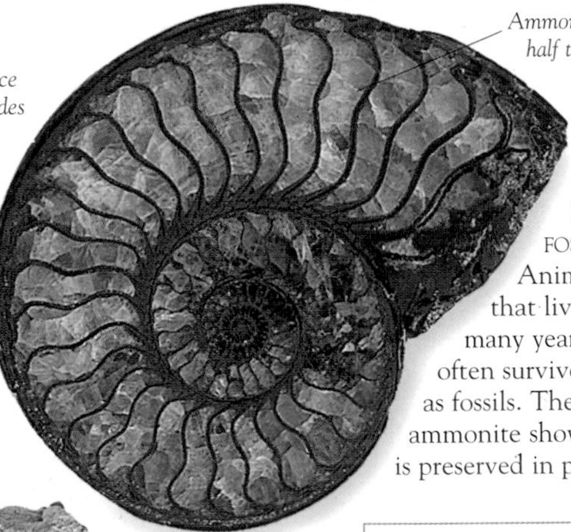

Ammonite cut in half to show its insides

PYRITE CRYSTAL
There are several forms of pyrite crystal. Cubes are common, but this sample from the Italian island of Elba has 12 five-sided faces. The shape of the crystal depends on its growing conditions.

PYRITE FOSSILS
Animals that lived many years ago often survive today as fossils. The ammonite shown here is preserved in pyrite.

Spear-shaped crystals in chalk

MARCASITE
Although the same elements that make up pyrite are found in marcasite, this mineral is less stable and decays in air. Newly found fossils made of marcasite crumble to dust if they are not properly cared for.

PYRITE FACTS
• Hardness: 6–6.5
• SG: 5
• Color: brassy to pale yellow
• Black streak
• Opaque
• Metallic luster

CHALCOPYRITE

An important metal ore, chalcopyrite has a more brassy color than pyrite and is much softer. This sample is made up of twinned crystals that have formed with white quartz.

Quartz crystals

COPPER ORE

This 19th-century diving helmet is made of copper, a metal that is extracted from chalcopyrite.

Lines, called striations, that form as crystals grow

Pale yellow color

CUBIC

CUBIC PYRITE

MALACHITE AND AZURITE

COPPER ROOFS TURN GREEN in the open air. The green material is malachite, which is an altered form of copper. When malachite replaces copper in ores underground, the mineral itself becomes a copper ore. It is then called a secondary ore. Azurite is also a secondary ore of copper. It has a characteristic bright blue color.

POLISHED MALACHITE
Bands of color make up this polished malachite slab. Malachite is a popular decorative material that is used in buildings and ornaments. It takes a good polish, but dulls quickly because it is soft.

Specimen with typical dark green color and botryoidal habit

MONOCLINIC

ALTERED MINERAL
Copper minerals near the Earth's surface alter when exposed to water and cool temperatures. Malachite often forms in these conditions. Common habits are botryoidal lumps and tiny crystals. It always has a green color, which varies only in intensity.

Malachite is widely
used as a decorative
stone. It is also
a secondary ore
of copper

MALACHITE FACTS

- Hardness: 3.5–4
- SG: 4
- Color: green
- Pale green streak
- Translucent to opaque
- Glassy or silky luster

Powdered
malachite

Powdered azurite

GREEN AND BLUE
Malachite and azurite
produce natural pigments. Bright
green malachite pigment was known
in ancient Egypt. Azurite grinds down
to give a rich color called azure blue.

Azurite
crystals

Tiny malachite
crystals form a crust

AZURITE
Vivid blue azurite has almost
the same chemical makeup
as malachite, but contains less
water. These two minerals often
grow together, as they have done here.

Limonite

69

OLIVINE

THE NAME OLIVINE refers to a group of minerals that are found in igneous rocks. This group only forms in molten rock beneath the Earth's surface. Peridot is the best-known variety of olivine. It is a gemstone with an olive-green color and oily luster. The finest peridot specimens come from Zebirget in the Red Sea.

PERIDOT
CRYSTALS

PERIDOT
Gem-quality olivine is known as peridot. The ancient Greeks and Romans were among the first people to use this mineral for decoration.

OLIVINE FACTS

- Hardness: 6.5–7
- SG: 3.27–4.32
- Color: green or brown
- White streak
- Transparent to translucent
- Oily or glassy luster

Mass of forsterite crystals

FORSTERITE
Olivine contains varying amounts of iron and magnesium. The variety that only has magnesium present is called forsterite. This mineral can exist on its own, but it can also form a rock called dunite.

PELE'S
HAIR

WIRY ROCK
Golden-brown "Pele's hair" is a
remarkable wiry rock made up of
tiny olivine crystals enclosed in
threads of basalt glass. It forms
during volcanic eruptions.

VOLCANIC BOMBS
An erupting volcano tosses volcanic bombs into
the night sky above the New Hebrides Islands
in the Pacific Ocean. The bombs are sticky
blobs of lava that harden into rock.
They can be broken open
to reveal green
olivine crystals.

Distinctive
oily luster

TRANSPARENT
PERIDOT

ORTHORHOMBIC

Peridot with a deep
green color is the most
valuable

71

TOURMALINE

THE RANGE OF COLOR seen in tourmaline is the greatest of any mineral. Even a single crystal can have several colors. This mineral develops its complex chemistry in igneous and metamorphic regions. It also forms in mineral veins. Tourmaline can grow with other minerals such as beryl, quartz, and feldspar.

GREEN CRYSTAL
Different colors of tourmaline have different names. The green variety, shown here set in a mass of feldspar crystals, is called chromdravite. Pink rubellite and multicolored elbaite are other important varieties.

TRIGONAL/
HEXAGONAL

Mass of feldspar

LIKE A WATERMELON
This example is known as "watermelon" tourmaline because its colors are similar to those of the fruit. Impurities cause the colors in the crystal.

72

BLACK TOURMALINE
Schorl is the black variety of tourmaline. It is a common mineral in granite pegmatites and often occurs with quartz, feldspars, and micas. Iron-rich schorl crystals often have parallel grooves running down their sides. The specimen shown here is made up of schorl and white quartz crystals.

Schorl

Quartz

Poorly formed schorl crystals

JOHN RUSKIN

CHEMISTRY
The English philosopher John Ruskin (1819–1900) described the chemistry of tourmaline as being "... more like a medieval doctor's prescription than the making of a respectable mineral!"

TOURMALINE FACTS
- Hardness: 7–7.5
- SG: 3–3.2
- Color: green; can be many other colors
- White streak
- Transparent to translucent
- Glassy luster

PLEOCHROISM
Tourmaline is a pleochroic mineral. This means that it looks a different color when viewed from different angles. This crystal, for example, appears green from the side. But it would appear black if you could turn it and look at it from the top.

73

JADE

TOUGHER THAN STEEL, but soft enough to be carved, jade is rare and precious. Tools and weapons were its earliest uses. Later, it was made into jewelry and ornaments. In 1863, the French scientist Damour showed that two different minerals shared the name jade. These minerals are called jadeite and nephrite.

JADEITE
A member of the pyroxene mineral group, jadeite forms in metamorphic rocks. The most valuable jadeite is known as "imperial jade."

Jadeite is an excellent carving material.

CARVED NEPHRITE
Both types of jade are excellent carving stones. They are tough materials that rarely crack or splinter because they consist of masses of tiny grains and fibers. This Maori "tiki," or good luck ornament, is made of nephrite.

MONOCLINIC

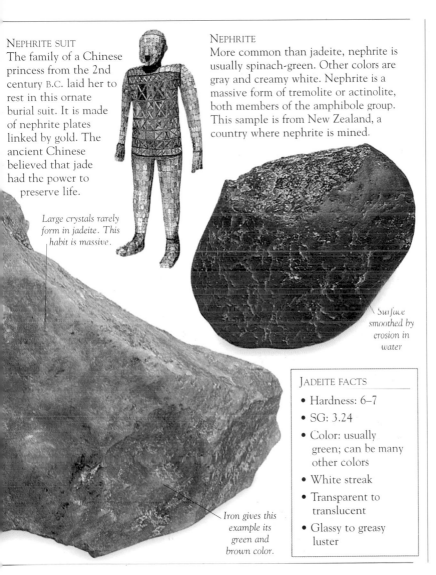

NEPHRITE SUIT

The family of a Chinese princess from the 2nd century B.C. laid her to rest in this ornate burial suit. It is made of nephrite plates linked by gold. The ancient Chinese believed that jade had the power to preserve life.

Large crystals rarely form in jadeite. This habit is massive.

NEPHRITE

More common than jadeite, nephrite is usually spinach-green. Other colors are gray and creamy white. Nephrite is a massive form of tremolite or actinolite, both members of the amphibole group. This sample is from New Zealand, a country where nephrite is mined.

Surface smoothed by erosion in water

JADEITE FACTS

- Hardness: 6–7
- SG: 3.24
- Color: usually green; can be many other colors
- White streak
- Transparent to translucent
- Glassy to greasy luster

Iron gives this example its green and brown color.

COPPER

THE FIRST METAL to be separated from its ore and put to use was probably copper. People have worked this metal into weapons and tools for 8,000 years. It can be used on its own, or mixed with other metals like zinc and tin to form alloys.

COPPER ORNAMENT

Copper rarely forms as a native mineral, and most commonly occurs in deposits of chalcopyrite.

NATIVE COPPER
A dendritic habit is typical of native copper. Fresh copper is a pale rose-red color, but it tarnishes quickly to copper-brown in contact with air.

Bundle of copper wires

NATIVE COPPER FACTS

- Hardness: 2.5–3
- SG: 8.9
- Color: copper-red or pale rose-red
- Copper-red streak
- Opaque
- Metallic luster

CYPRUS COPPER
The Mediterranean island of Cyprus, shown here, was the site of some of the earliest copper mines.

DEEP-SEA CABLE
An excellent carrier of electricity, copper is stretched into wires and used in deep-sea cables.

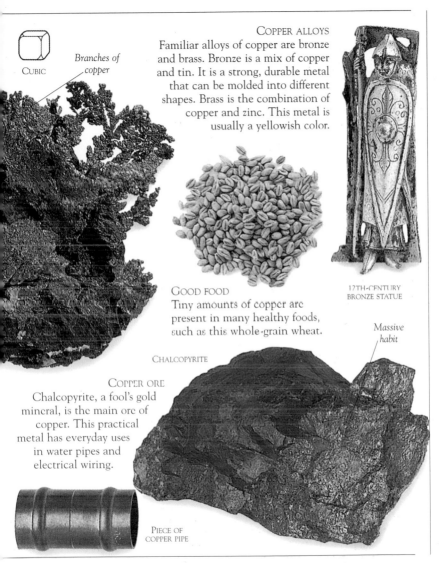

CUBIC

Branches of copper

COPPER ALLOYS

Familiar alloys of copper are bronze and brass. Bronze is a mix of copper and tin. It is a strong, durable metal that can be molded into different shapes. Brass is the combination of copper and zinc. This metal is usually a yellowish color.

GOOD FOOD

Tiny amounts of copper are present in many healthy foods, such as this whole-grain wheat.

12TH-CENTURY BRONZE STATUE

CHALCOPYRITE

Massive habit

COPPER ORE

Chalcopyrite, a fool's gold mineral, is the main ore of copper. This practical metal has everyday uses in water pipes and electrical wiring.

PIECE OF COPPER PIPE

HEMATITE

KIDNEY-SHAPED LUMPS and
shiny black crystals are
both common forms
of hematite. This
mineral is prized as
an iron ore and
as a gemstone.
It develops
in many
rocks, from
granites to
limestones.

ROUNDED MASSES
The typical form of hematite is rounded
masses, which look like animal kidneys.
The name of this habit is reniform, from
the Latin word for kidneys.

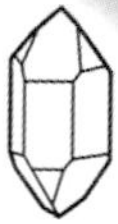

*Metallic
luster*

TRIGONAL/
HEXAGONAL

REDDISH-BROWN PIGMENT
Ground hematite makes a
reddish-brown pigment called
ocher. It is one of the oldest
natural pigments.

CHINESE MEDICINE
Some Chinese
doctors treat their
patients with powdered hematite
mixed with red clay. They believe it
is a useful medicine for certain illnesses.

HEMATITE FACTS

• Hardness: 5–6
• SG: 5.26
• Color: dull red or
  shiny black
  • Red streak
  • Opaque
  • Metallic to earthy
    luster

Iridescent
hematite
crystals

Stone lining
hides steel
framework

IRIDESCENCE
These hematite crystals from
Elba show iridescence. It is
caused by light bouncing off
thin chemical films on the
surface of the crystals.

Hexagonal
(six-sided)
crystals

Another name
for reniform
hematite is
kidney ore

SHINY SURFACE
This sample is
called specular
hematite, a semi-
precious form of
the mineral. The word
specular describes crystals
with shiny, reflective surfaces.

STRONG STEEL
Hematite is an ore of iron.
This tough metal has
many uses on its own, but
is often converted to steel.
Strong and flexible, steel
is used in buildings such as
the Empire State Building
in New York.

79

CASSITERITE

MOST PEOPLE HAVE heard of tin. It is a common metal that has uses in industry and the home. The main ore of tin is cassiterite, a mineral that occurs in many parts of the world. Cassiterite forms in high-temperature hydrothermal veins and metamorphic rocks.

CRYSTALLINE CASSITERITE
Although cassiterite is a metal ore, it is unusual because it does not look metallic. Instead of being dull and opaque, crystals are shiny and translucent.

TETRAGONAL

GEMSTONES
Jewelers regard cassiterite as a semiprecious gemstone. Its qualities include hardness (between 6 and 7 on Mohs' scale) and the ability to hold a good polish. But even the finest cassiterite gems have flaws that affect their color – and hence their value.

SUPPLIES OF TIN
Disused buildings, such as this engine house, are all that remain of the tin mining industry in Cornwall, England. Up until the 19th-century, the area was one of the most important sources of the metal. Its mines had operated for thousands of years. Today, Southeast Asia and West Africa supply most of the world's tin.

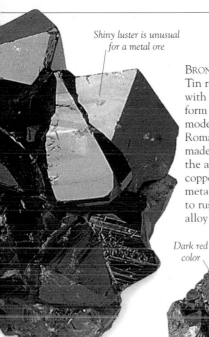

Shiny luster is unusual for a metal ore

BRONZE HELMET
Tin readily mixes with other metals to form alloys. This modern replica of a Roman helmet is made from bronze, the alloy of tin and copper. It is a strong metal that is resistant to rust. Pewter is the alloy of tin and lead.

LEGIONARY
HELMET (C. 50 B.C.)

Dark red color

Mass of twinned crystals

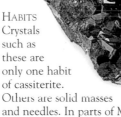

CASSITERITE FACTS

- Hardness: 6–7
- SG: 7
- Color: brown or black
- Dirty white streak
- Transparent to almost opaque
- Greasy to bright luster

HABITS
Crystals such as these are only one habit of cassiterite. Others are solid masses and needles. In parts of Mexico, this mineral occurs as raspberry-shaped lumps known as wood tin.

Rock on which crystals have grown

MERCURY MINERALS

NATIVE MERCURY IS liquid at room temperature and is poisonous. Despite these curious properties, this metal has many commercial uses and is widely mined. Mercury can occur as a native element, but is most common in the mineral cinnabar.

Cinnabar is easily identified by its bright red color

CINNABAR

Highly poisonous cinnabar is the main ore of mercury. This bright red mineral forms around volcanic vents and hot springs. It also occurs in mineral veins. Spain, Italy, and China have the largest cinnabar deposits.

Greasy luster

TRIGONAL/
HEXAGONAL

CINNABAR FACTS

- Hardness: 2–2.5
- SG: 8–8.2
- Color: red to brown
- Reddish-brown to scarlet streak
- Transparent to opaque
- Greasy or earthy luster

VERMILION

Cinnabar is the main ingredient in the pigment vermilion. First used for painting in ancient China, its brilliant orange-red color was at the height of its popularity in the Middle Ages. Today's paints are usually made from less poisonous substances.

THERMOMETER
Mercury's best-known use is in thermometers. These tools consist of a glass tube containing liquid mercury and a temperature scale. When the thermometer heats up, the mercury expands and rises up the tube. A reading can then be taken off the scale. This thermometer dates from the 18th-century.

Bulb full of mercury

NATIVE MERCURY
At room temperature, mercury forms small blobs of silvery liquid. As a result, it is rarely found in its native state. Small deposits do occur, however, in rock cavities around volcanic vents. Native mercury is opaque and has a bright metallic luster. Its high density is another identifying feature.

CLOSE-UP OF DEPOSIT OF NATIVE MERCURY IN ROCK CAVITY

SPHALERITE

THE MOST COMMON ORE of zinc is sphalerite. Also known as blende or "black jack," this mineral forms in hydrothermal veins with other ores such as galena. Some sphalerite is gem quality, but it is often too soft for a cut to last. The best stones have a deep reddish-brown color.

SPHALERITE GEMSTONE

UNCUT SPHALERITE
Sphalerite crystals such as this one are valued for their fine colors. After cutting, however, they wear down quickly and lose their sparkle.

MASSIVE SPHALERITE

CUBIC

WORTHLESS MINERAL?
Early lead miners thought sphalerite to be worthless and threw it away. Now that its value is known, disused lead mines are reopening so that the sphalerite can be recovered.

84

Oysters are a good source of zinc

SOURCES OF ZINC
Ores like sphalerite are not the only places where zinc is found. It also occurs in many foods.
Good sources of zinc are eggs, whole-grain cereals, nuts, and seafood.

BUILDING MATERIAL
Galvanization is a major use of zinc. This is the process of coating iron and steel with zinc to protect them from rust. Zinc does not corrode (wear away or rust) easily, and is occasionally used as a building material.

French bell-tower coated with zinc

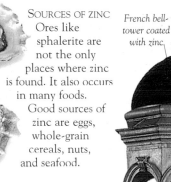

Rough surface

Working parts made from steel, a tougher metal than brass

METAL ALLOY
Brass is an alloy of zinc and copper. An attractive metal that takes a good polish, brass is often used for decoration. The protective case of this watch is made from brass.

SPHALERITE FACTS

- Hardness: 3.5–4
- SG: 3.9–4.1
- Color: brown or red; can be many other colors
- White streak
- Transparent to translucent
- Greasy luster

GARNET

A GROUP OF silica-based minerals, garnets occur the world over, especially in metamorphic rocks. Geologists use garnets to identify rocks that have been altered by heat and pressure. A more common use is in jewelry. Purplish-red pyrope and red almandine garnets are most prized by jewelers.

Mass of twinned crystals

GROSSULAR GARNET
Pink and orange are common colors of grossular garnet, which is the lightest-colored variety of garnet.

Similar color to garnet

POMEGRANATE AND SEEDS

CUBIC

SIMILAR COLOR
The name garnet may come from the Latin word for pomegranate, *granatum*. You can easily see the similarity of the colors of the glossy gemstones and the seeds of the fruit.

GROSSULAR GARNET FACTS

- Hardness: 6.5–7
- SG: 3.4–3.6
- Color: red or brown; can be many other colors
- White streak
- Transparent to opaque
- Dull to glassy luster

SUTTON HOO PURSE
This purse lid inlaid with garnet was among the jewels found on a 7th-century burial ship at Sutton Hoo, Suffolk, England.

Rounded grains are a typical habit of pyrope

PYROPE
These rounded red stones are pyrope garnets. They form in igneous rocks that contain very little silica. Some of the best pyrope comes from the former Czechoslovakia.

Almandine forms in metamorphic rocks like schist

POPULAR GEMSTONE
Since Roman times, almandine garnet has been a popular choice for jewelry. Deep red crystals, like the one shown here, have the highest value.

ALMANDINE GARNET

FLUORITE

THE COMMERCIAL VALUE of fluorite comes from its ability to melt easily. The origin of its name is also related to this property. It is derived from the Latin word *fluere*, which means "to flow." Fluorite is a common mineral that is found in hydrothermal veins and limestones.

COLORS OF FLUORITE
Purple cubes of fluorite are distinctive and widespread. This mineral also occurs in green, pink, and blue, but its only habits are crystalline or granular.

This green fluorite appears purple in ultraviolet light

BLUE JOHN
Banded fluorite is known as Blue John. Its other name is Derbyshire Spar, after the English county in which it occurs. The bands vary in color from blue and purple to yellow.

FLUORESCENCE
When invisible ultraviolet light shines on fluorite, the crystals appear to give off visible light in return. This is fluorescence. The fluorescent color of fluorite is often different from its daylight color.

FLUORITE FACTS

- Hardness: 4
- SG: 3.18
- Color: purple; can be many other colors
- White streak
- Transparent to translucent
- Glassy luster

FLUORITE IN STEELMAKING

An important industrial use of fluorite is in steelmaking. It is added to the molten metal to help it flow easily. At the same time, it removes impurities like sulfur and phosphorus. This worker is overseeing the steelmaking process at a plant in Port Talbot, South Wales.

Glassy luster

Transparency around edges of crystal

PURPLE FLUORITE

CUBIC

Fluorite crystals often form as clusters of twins. Twins are cubic, which means they have six faces.

INSCRIBED
TURQUOISE ORNAMENT

TURQUOISE

FEW MINERALS HAVE been popular for as long as turquoise. First mined more than 6,000 years ago in the Sinai Desert in the Middle East, it is one of the best-known precious stones. Indeed, many people use the term "turquoise blue" to describe a certain shade of blue-green.

NATIVE TURQUOISE

Turquoise is a water-rich mineral that forms only in dry regions of the world. It develops in fine-grained masses, but never as large crystals. The finest turquoise comes from Iran, where it has been mined for 3,000 years.

Crystals with dull luster

CARVING TURQUOISE

Most of the world's turquoise deposits are in the southwestern United States. Over many centuries, people from the region have built up a reputation for carving attractive jewelry from local rock. This Native American worker from New Mexico carries on the tradition.

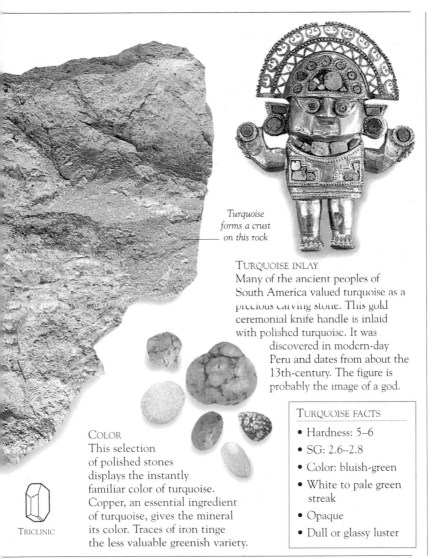

Turquoise forms a crust on this rock

TURQUOISE INLAY

Many of the ancient peoples of South America valued turquoise as a precious carving stone. This gold ceremonial knife handle is inlaid with polished turquoise. It was discovered in modern-day Peru and dates from about the 13th-century. The figure is probably the image of a god.

COLOR

This selection of polished stones displays the instantly familiar color of turquoise. Copper, an essential ingredient of turquoise, gives the mineral its color. Traces of iron tinge the less valuable greenish variety.

TRICLINIC

TURQUOISE FACTS

- Hardness: 5–6
- SG: 2.6–2.8
- Color: bluish-green
- White to pale green streak
- Opaque
- Dull or glassy luster

LAZURITE

THE MAIN INGREDIENT of ultramarine, the brilliant blue pigment, is lazurite. This mineral also dominates lapis lazuli, a rock prized for carvings and jewelry for thousands of years. Lazurite has a massive habit and is rare in nature. It is a metamorphic mineral that only occurs in marble.

NATIVE LAZURITE

A brilliant blue color characterizes native lazurite. The color comes from sulfur atoms, which are an essential part of its makeup. Lazurite is a silica-based mineral that develops in masses as heat alters limestone to marble.

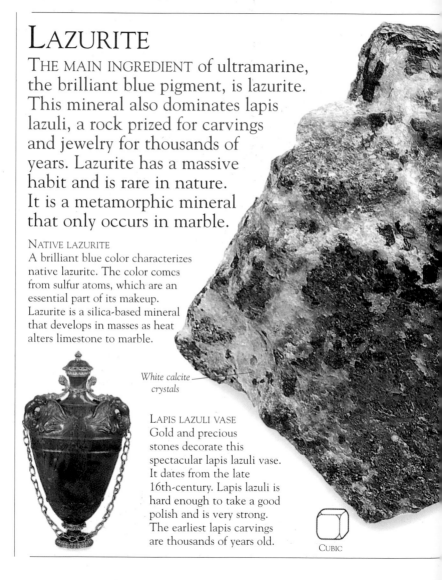

White calcite crystals

LAPIS LAZULI VASE

Gold and precious stones decorate this spectacular lapis lazuli vase. It dates from the late 16th-century. Lapis lazuli is hard enough to take a good polish and is very strong. The earliest lapis carvings are thousands of years old.

CUBIC

Sulfur gives lazurite its color

LAPIS LAZULI NECKLACE

Carved beads

LAZURITE FACTS

- Hardness: 5–5.5
- SG: 2.4–2.5
- Color: blue
- Blue streak
- Nearly opaque
- Dull or glassy luster

Paint made from ultramarine pigment

ULTRAMARINE
The ancient Persians were the first people to crush lapis lazuli and use it to make ultramarine.

Rough lapis lazuli with a high lazurite content

Traces of brass-colored pyrite

UNCUT LAPIS LAZULI
Lapis lazuli consists of masses of lazurite mixed with calcite and pyrite. The higher the content of lazurite, the more precious the lapis.

Patches of blue lazurite

MAGNETITE

THE ANCIENT CHINESE MADE their first compasses from magnetite, an iron oxide that has natural magnetism. This mineral was also known to the ancient Greeks, who called it lodestone. Today, magnetite is important as an iron ore. It occurs in small quantities in many igneous rock and meteorites. Some volcanic bombs also contain magnetite.

MAGNETITE CRYSTAL
Eight triangular faces make up this shiny magnetite crystal. Other habits of this mineral are massive and granular. Magnetite is a hard, heavy substance that does not fuse with other minerals. It does not cleave easily.

MAGNETIC COMPASS
Natural magnetism is one of the key identification features of magnetite. Magnetic materials attract small pieces of iron. They also deflect the needle of a compass. Seafarers have used magnetic compasses since the 12th-century.

Compass point

MAGNETITE FACTS
- Hardness: 5.5–6.5
- SG: 5.2
- Color: black
- Black streak
- Opaque
- Metallic luster on fresh faces

LARGE DEPOSIT
Magnetite contains about 70 percent iron, making it a rich metal ore. One of the largest deposits of this mineral is at Kiruna, Sweden. Snow covers the huge open-cast workings at Kiruna in this picture.

FORGED METAL

Iron is valuable once separated from its ore. The Romans forged iron into weapons and armor. Forging is the process of beating heated metal into shape.

ROMAN LEGIONARY ARMOR

Iron plates held together by leather straps

CUBIC

Thousands of small grains make up this sample of magnetite.

Dull, metallic luster

AMPHIBOLES

JUST LIKE DETECTIVES, geologists search for clues in the rocks they study. A typical "investigation" may begin with a group of minerals called amphiboles. These rock-forming minerals are useful to geologists because they record the conditions of temperature and pressure deep inside the Earth.

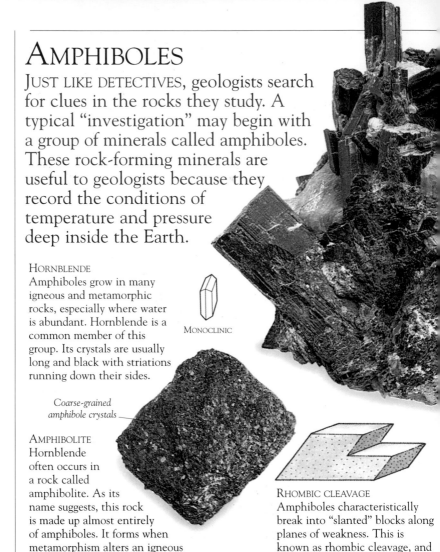

HORNBLENDE
Amphiboles grow in many igneous and metamorphic rocks, especially where water is abundant. Hornblende is a common member of this group. Its crystals are usually long and black with striations running down their sides.

MONOCLINIC

Coarse-grained amphibole crystals

AMPHIBOLITE
Hornblende often occurs in a rock called amphibolite. As its name suggests, this rock is made up almost entirely of amphiboles. It forms when metamorphism alters an igneous rock such as dolerite.

RHOMBIC CLEAVAGE
Amphiboles characteristically break into "slanted" blocks along planes of weakness. This is known as rhombic cleavage, and is shown in this simple diagram.

WHITE AMPHIBOLE
Tremolite forms in marble and serpentinite (an igneous rock). Large deposits may be mined for a type of asbestos called mountain leather. This white tremolite sample has a plumose, or feather-like, habit.

GLAUCOPHANE
Sheaves of fibers and granular masses are the usual habits of glaucophane. This amphibole only forms in low temperatures and high pressures, usually as very hot rocks cool down. It often has a violet color.

Striations on side of twinned hornblende crystal

INTERLOCKING CRYSTALS
A common habit of riebeckite, shown here, is masses of long, interlocking crystals. They are usually dark blue to black in color. Riebeckite also occurs as bunches of fibers (known as crocidolite), which can be mined for asbestos.

HORNBLENDE FACTS

- Hardness: 5–6
- SG: 3.28–3.41
- Color: usually black; can be green and greenish-brown
- White streak
- Translucent to opaque
- Silky to glassy luster

97

PYROXENES

THE MINERALS IN the pyroxene group are vital rock formers on Earth. They occur in igneous rocks, such as basalt, and make up most of the Earth's mantle. These minerals also form in metamorphic regions. And if you could get there, you would find pyroxenes in the rocks on the Moon.

MONOCLINIC

AUGITE
The most common pyroxene is augite. It is a green to black mineral that forms in many basalts and gabbros. Augite rarely develops large crystals such as the one shown here, which comes from Italy.

Augite crystal

Rock mass made of small crystals

PLATINUM MINE
This South African platinum mine is on the world's most valuable mineral lode (vein of metal ore). The lode cuts through pyroxenite, a rock entirely made up of pyroxenes.

AUGITE FACTS

- Hardness: 5.5–6
- SG: 3.23–3.52
- Color: black; can be various shades of brown and green
- Grayish-green streak
- Transparent to translucent
- Dull to glassy luster

ENSTATITE
Meteorites and rocks in the Earth's mantle are rich in enstatite. This pyroxene often develops as fibers, but the specimen shown here has a crystalline habit. The crystals are translucent with a dark gray color.

DIOPSIDE
Dark green crystals with a glassy or pearly luster are a usual form of diopside. This mineral is the pyroxene most commonly found in metamorphic rocks. It also occurs in igneous rocks like basalt and gabbro.

Well-formed
green crystals

Striations on
side of long
crystal

AEGIRINE
Crystals and fibrous masses are the usual habits of aegirine. This is a quite rare pyroxene that occurs in igneous and metamorphic rocks. Like all the other pyroxenes, aegirine has two cleavage planes that cross each other at right angles.

ROCKS

IGNEOUS ROCKS

HOT, LIQUID MAGMA from the Earth's crust or mantle solidifies to form igneous rock. There are two main types of igneous rock – intrusive and extrusive. The intrusive type forms underground. Extrusive igneous rocks solidify at the Earth's surface.

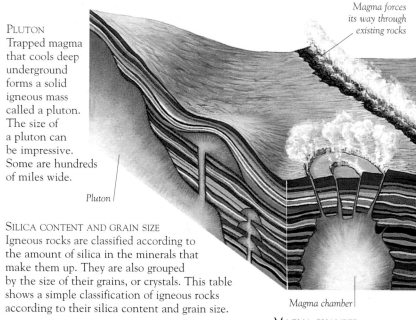

Magma forces its way through existing rocks

PLUTON
Trapped magma that cools deep underground forms a solid igneous mass called a pluton. The size of a pluton can be impressive. Some are hundreds of miles wide.

Pluton

Magma chamber

SILICA CONTENT AND GRAIN SIZE
Igneous rocks are classified according to the amount of silica in the minerals that make them up. They are also grouped by the size of their grains, or crystals. This table shows a simple classification of igneous rocks according to their silica content and grain size.

	HIGH SILICA	LOW SILICA
SMALL GRAINS	Obsidian	Basalt
MEDIUM GRAINS	Microgranite	Dolerite
LARGE GRAINS	Granite	Gabbro

MAGMA CHAMBER
Large underground magma chambers feed volcanoes at the Earth's surface. When these chambers cool, they solidify to form plutons.

GRANITE AND OBSIDIAN

Magma is the raw material of igneous rocks. It can come from the Earth's crust or directly from the mantle. Two rocks from the same magma source can look very different, however. Magma from an underground chamber cooled at the Earth's surface to form this block of obsidian. The granite specimen developed when the same chamber cooled to form a pluton.

Granite is an intrusive igneous rock. It has large crystals because it formed from magma that cooled slowly.

Layers of lava

Obsidian is an extrusive igneous rock. It forms as lava cools very rapidly.

Sill

Volcano

Dyke

SILL

Magma can slide between the bedding planes (layers) of sedimentary rocks. When this magma cools and hardens, it forms a feature called a sill. After erosion, sills appear at the Earth's surface as flat plates.

VOLCANO

Magma at the Earth's surface is called lava. It emerges through erupting volcanoes. The makeup of magma affects the type of eruption. The higher the silica content of magma, the more violent the eruption.

DYKE

When magma breaks through existing rock structures, it may cool to form a dyke. This type of feature may form from the tube, or fissure, that links a magma chamber to a volcano.

103

GRANITE

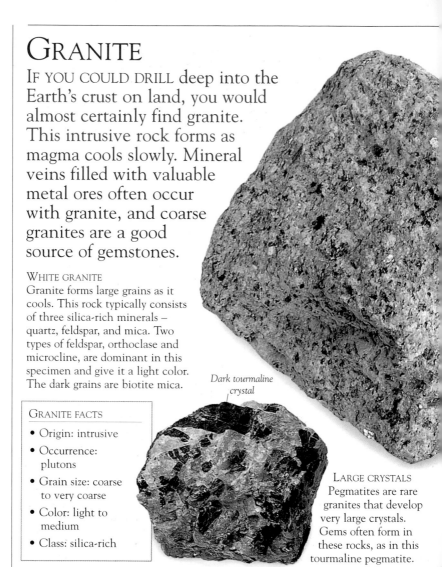

IF YOU COULD DRILL deep into the Earth's crust on land, you would almost certainly find granite. This intrusive rock forms as magma cools slowly. Mineral veins filled with valuable metal ores often occur with granite, and coarse granites are a good source of gemstones.

WHITE GRANITE
Granite forms large grains as it cools. This rock typically consists of three silica-rich minerals – quartz, feldspar, and mica. Two types of feldspar, orthoclase and microcline, are dominant in this specimen and give it a light color. The dark grains are biotite mica.

Dark tourmaline crystal

GRANITE FACTS

- Origin: intrusive
- Occurrence: plutons
- Grain size: coarse to very coarse
- Color: light to medium
- Class: silica-rich

LARGE CRYSTALS
Pegmatites are rare granites that develop very large crystals. Gems often form in these rocks, as in this tourmaline pegmatite.

104

Large crystals formed as magma cooled slowly

GRANITE LANDFORMS
Tors are typical granite landforms that look like huge boulders stacked on top of each other. They became exposed as the surrounding rocks eroded away. This tor is on Dartmoor, in southwest England.

GRAPHIC GRANITE
Graphic granite contains strange gray quartz crystals. They have shapes like letters in an alphabet and form a series of lines. Graphic granite develops as magma cools under pressure.

Aligned quartz crystals

PINK GRANITE
Orthoclase feldspar dominates pink granite and gives this rock its color. Attractive granites such as this are commonly used as building stones, usually as polished decorative slabs. Crushed granite serves as a gravel and road-building material.

Pink orthoclase feldspar

CARVING STONE
Granite is a hard-wearing rock that carves well. This statue of the Egyptian pharaoh Rameses II was carved from blocks of dark-colored granite.

105

OBSIDIAN AND RHYOLITE

VIOLENT EXPLOSIONS precede the formation of obsidian and rhyolite. These extrusive rocks form when magma with the same chemical makeup as granite reaches the Earth's surface. This magma is rich in silica, which makes it viscous (sticky). It traps gas that builds up and eventually causes a violent eruption.

OBSIDIAN

A simple way to describe obsidian is to call it "granite glass." Everyday glass, which is made from quartz sand, is a good comparison. Obsidian forms when lava cools so rapidly that crystals do not have time to grow.

Scattered snowflakes

SNOWFLAKE OBSIDIAN

White fibrous crystals can develop in obsidian, especially if the rock comes into contact with water. The crystals resemble snowflakes, giving this example its name.

OBSIDIAN FACTS

- Origin: extrusive
- Occurrence: volcanic
- Grain size: fine
- Color: black
- Class: silica-rich

Obsidian is usually black

SCATTERED LAVA
The sulfur-rich springs at Rotorua, New Zealand, are the remains of a huge eruption. A gas cloud surged into the air, scattering lava all over the area. The lava hardened into rhyolite.

The bands in rhyolite often have different colors. The crystals that make it up are too small to be seen with the naked eye.

BANDED RHYOLITE
Rhyolite consists of swirls of crystals and glassy material. The crystals are fine-grained and include quartz, feldspar, and mica. The bands in this specimen formed as lava flowed short distances after the eruption that brought it to the Earth's surface.

Smooth, glassy surface

OBSIDIAN SPEARHEAD
Fragments of obsidian have razor-sharp edges. They are also hard. These two properties made obsidian an ideal rock for early weapons, such as this spearhead. It is from the Admiralty Islands, near Papua New Guinea.

Obsidian blade

GABBRO

A DEEP-LEVEL EXPLORATION of the Earth's crust beneath the oceans would reveal solid layers of gabbro. This coarse-grained rock forms when magma from the mantle cools. Rock collectors value gabbro specimens because the rock is relatively uncommon on land.

MINERAL MAKEUP
Gabbro is a silica-poor intrusive rock. It usually consists of feldspar, olivine, and members of the pyroxene group. Pyroxenes give this example its dark color. The light grains are a type of feldspar called plagioclase. Mineral veins are often found near gabbro masses in the Earth's crust.

Different minerals form light and dark layers

GABBRO FACTS

- Origin: intrusive
- Occurrence: plutons
- Grain size: coarse
- Color: medium to dark
- Class: silica-poor

LAYERED GABBRO
Some gabbros form in layers made of single minerals. Magnetite makes up the dark layers in this specimen. The light parts are plagioclase feldspar.

ECLOGITE

A particularly silica-poor variety of gabbro is called eclogite. This rock is dominated by pyroxenes and garnet. These minerals form medium to coarse grains, and banding often occurs in the rock. Geologists think that eclogite resembles the chemical makeup of rocks in the Earth's mantle.

Banding in eclogite

Dark, coarse-grained pyroxenes

SERPENTINITE

Gabbros and eclogite break down in air and water over time. The remains of the minerals that made them up form a range of clays, which make up serpentinite. This rock varies in color from green to red. It is fine-grained and often has bands. The green flakes in this example are the mineral serpentine.

GABBRO LANDSCAPE
The Black Cuillins of Skye, Scotland, consist of gabbro. These mountains have jagged ridges and steep sides. The rocks that make them up developed about 60 million years ago as the Atlantic Ocean formed.

BASALT AND DOLERITE

VIOLENT VOLCANIC eruptions are quite rare.
Most eruptions are rather gentle events.
Lava from the gentler volcanoes is
runny and hardens into basalt
and dolerite. These rocks are
fine-grained equivalents of
gabbro. They are also the
most common rocks in
the Earth's crust.

BASALT
Minerals that make up
basalt include feldspars,
pyroxenes, and olivine. They
typically give this extrusive
rock a dark-gray to black color.
The crystals in basalt are tiny.

*Large
crystal*

PORPHYRITIC
BASALT
Large crystals
can form in
basalt. They start
to grow before they
reach the Earth's
surface in erupting
lava. As the lava
cools, a mass of
smaller crystals
traps the large crystals.
They form a rock called
porphyritic basalt.

BASALT FACTS
- Origin: extrusive
- Occurrence: volcanic
- Grain size: fine
- Color: dark
- Class: silica-poor

You can see the crystals in dolerite with the naked eye.

DOLERITE
A layer of dolerite lies beneath the basalt on the ocean floors. Dolerite is an intrusive rock that usually forms in the Earth's crust. It has coarser grains than basalt.

HAWAIIAN VOLCANO
The Kilauea volcano in Hawaii is a basalt volcano. It erupts almost continuously, but without great explosions.

HOLES LEFT BY GAS BUBBLES
As lava hardens into basalt, gas bubbles can leave rounded holes on the surface of the rock. The holes are called vesicles.

GIANT'S CAUSEWAY
Basalt can form many-sided columns as it cools. These columns are part of the Giant's Causeway, Northern Ireland.

Rounded vesicles in basalt

111

ROCKS FROM SPACE

OUR MOON, THE PLANETS, meteorites, and comets all consist of rocks and minerals. Rocks from space are clearly difficult to collect, but the effort is worthwhile because these rocks give us clues about the way the Earth formed about 4,600 million years ago.

STONY IRON
Meteorites fall to Earth from space. They are the remains of larger bodies that have broken up in the Earth's atmosphere. The example shown here is a stony iron meteorite. It is made up of silicate minerals, such as olivine, and a nickel-iron alloy.

Metallic appearance

MOON ROCK
Astronauts have returned to Earth with many samples of Moon rock. These rocks have been widely studied by geologists. The most common type of rock on the Moon is a variety of basalt that is also found on Earth. This astronaut is collecting rock and soil samples on the Moon.

COMMON METEORITES
Chondrites are the most common meteorites. They are also very old, forming at about the same time as the Earth. Chondrites mostly contain minerals such as olivine and pyroxenes.

Mass of small, rounded grains

Pits created by heating during meteorite's fall

COMET
Some meteorites may be the remains of comets. These are huge "snowballs" made of ice, rock fragments, and gases that move around the Sun. Their tails can be millions of miles long. This picture shows the comet Kohoutek.

TEKTITES
When a meteorite hits the Earth, the intense heat melts fragments of the crust. Small blobs of molten rock fly out from the impact site, which harden to form rocks called tektites.

Smooth, shiny surface

BARRINGER CRATER
An iron meteorite about 656 ft (200 m) across created the Barringer crater, Arizona. The crater is ⅘ mile (1.3 km) wide.

113

METAMORPHIC ROCKS

EXISTING ROCKS ALTERED by heat and pressure, or simply by heat alone, are called metamorphic rocks. The processes involved in metamorphism are slow. As the existing rocks are baked and crushed, new minerals gradually grow from the chemicals present and crystallize to form rock.

MAGMA CHAMBER

THERMAL METAMORPHISM

MAGMA CHAMBER
Metamorphism occurs in many different environments. For example, molten rock in a magma chamber is much hotter than the surrounding rocks. The heat from the magma chamber bakes these rocks, altering their form and mineral composition.

MARBLE

THERMAL METAMORPHISM
Rocks changed by the action of heat alone are called thermal, or contact, metamorphic rocks. This process occurs only where magma breaks into existing rock structures, such as in plutons, dykes, and sills. Marble is a thermal metamorphic rock.

INCREASING DEPTH
The deeper a rock is buried beneath the Earth's surface, the greater the heat and pressure that act on it. Heat increases because the mantle bakes the crust from below. Pressure increases because of the weight of the rocks above.

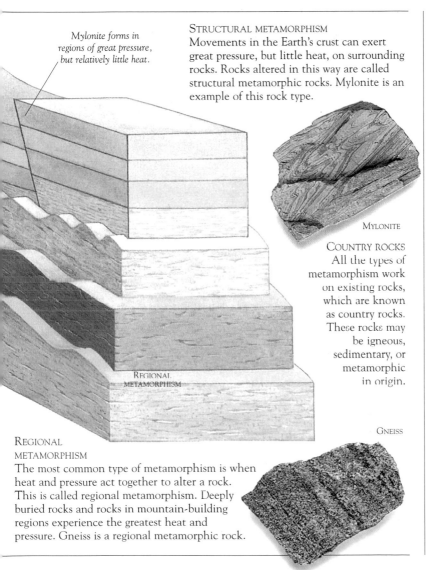

Mylonite forms in regions of great pressure, but relatively little heat.

STRUCTURAL METAMORPHISM

Movements in the Earth's crust can exert great pressure, but little heat, on surrounding rocks. Rocks altered in this way are called structural metamorphic rocks. Mylonite is an example of this rock type.

MYLONITE

COUNTRY ROCKS

All the types of metamorphism work on existing rocks, which are known as country rocks. These rocks may be igneous, sedimentary, or metamorphic in origin.

REGIONAL METAMORPHISM

GNEISS

REGIONAL METAMORPHISM

The most common type of metamorphism is when heat and pressure act together to alter a rock. This is called regional metamorphism. Deeply buried rocks and rocks in mountain-building regions experience the greatest heat and pressure. Gneiss is a regional metamorphic rock.

GNEISS AND SCHIST

METALWORKERS MAKE USEFUL objects by heating metal and beating it into shape. In a similar way, heat and pressure deep beneath the Earth's highest mountains turn old rocks into new. Rocks known as gneisses and schists form in these conditions. Gneiss (pronounced "nice") is forged in higher heat and pressure than schist, but both rocks develop bands called foliations.

FOLDED GNEISS
Gneiss forms under high pressure and heat. These conditions change the minerals in existing rocks into new minerals. Gneisses are coarse-grained rocks with minerals arranged in bands. Quartz and feldspar make up the light bands in this folded gneiss. The dark bands are hornblende and biotite mica.

GNEISS FACTS

- Origin: mountain ranges
- Grain size: medium to coarse
- Pressure: high
- Heat: high
- Class: regional

MIGMATITE
Rocks melt under very high heat and pressure. Migmatite is a coarse-grained rock that has partly melted, causing wavy, swirling patterns. If migmatite melts completely, it becomes a granite.

GARNETS IN SCHIST
Minerals with a hard, compact structure develop in gneisses and schists. This group of red almandine garnets, for example, formed in a light-colored mica schist.

Almandine garnet crystals

FOLDED SCHIST
Schists form in moderate heat and pressure. These rocks usually consist of medium-sized crystals arranged in parallel layers. The foliations in this example developed as pressure acted on the rock from different directions. Mica flakes give it a shiny surface.

GREAT BEAR LAKE
Gneiss is the oldest known rock and forms low-lying landscapes that are dotted with lakes. A good example of this type of a gneiss landscape is the area around Great Bear Lake, Canada.

Swirling patterns developed as rock partly melted in very high heat and pressure

Wavy bands of mica reflect light

117

SLATE

TAP A BLOCK of slate with a hammer and chisel and it will split into thin plates. This property makes slate an important roofing material and chalkboard surface. Slate forms when the minerals that make up fine-grained rocks, such as clay and shale, are changed into mica. This change takes place at the edges of mountain-building regions where pressure and heat are relatively low.

GREEN SLATE
Microscopic crystals of mica give slate its shiny, wet appearance. Another mineral, chlorite, colors the green specimen shown here. The dark specks are grains of carbon and pyrite.

ROOFING MATERIAL
Mica crystals in slate are arranged in layers. The rock breaks into flat sheets along these layers. Sheets of slate serve as a roofing material, as on this house in Spring Lake, New Jersey.

BLACK SLATE

Carbon and pyrite give this slate specimen a dark color. The larger pyrite crystals form parallel lines like words on a page. You can also see how this example consists of layers that are separated by cleavage planes.

A layer of slate ends at this slightly raised edge. There is a cleavage plane between each layer

SLATE QUARRY

Waste from a disused slate quarry near Blaenau Ffestiniog, North Wales, litters the hillside above this railway tunnel. Slate has been mined for centuries. Early miners used simple hammers and chisels to cut and split the rock.

SPOTTED SLATE

Most slate develops in mountain-building regions. Pre-existing slate may, however, be heated further by coming into contact with hot igneous rocks. This causes new minerals, such as cordierite and andalusite, to form in spotty patches.

Patches of randomly arranged cordierite

FOSSIL IN SLATE

Slate forms at such low temperatures and pressures that fossils survive from the original rocks. This example comes from Devon, England. It is known as a "Delabole butterfly."

SLATE FACTS

- Origin: mountain ranges
- Grain size: fine
- Pressure: low
- Heat: low
- Class: regional

MARBLE

THE ANCIENT GREEKS and Romans knew
the value of marble. They used this

MARBLE CAPITAL

perfect carving material to
craft some of their finest
statues and buildings.
Marble forms when
heat and pressure
alter limestone.
It is common
and occurs in mountain
areas all over the world.

*Coarse grains give a
sugary appearance*

WHITE MARBLE
Pure marble is white. It is the most prized
carving and building stone. This unpolished
specimen comes from near Malaga, Spain.
Known as Mijas marble, it consists of coarse grains.

*Colored
streaks*

GREEN MARBLE
Marble is altered
limestone. Impurities from
the limestone give marble
its many colors, including
red, pink, and green.
Marble may have only one
color, or many colors in
streaks or flowing patterns.

Greenish-brown olivine mixed with calcite

Marble consists of a mass of interlocking crystals. It is also a soft rock because it is largely made of calcite.

OLIVINE MARBLE
A variety of minerals form in marble if the heated limestone contained flint. For example, this marble specimen is rich in olivine, which is more commonly found in igneous rocks. The greenish-brown grains of olivine are easy to see.

Decorative marble arcading

MARBLE TOWER
The Campanile, or Leaning Tower, in Pisa, Italy, has marble panels, arcades, and columns. Italy has some of the world's finest marbles.

MARBLE FACTS

- Origin: where heat and pressure act on limestone
- Grain size: variable
- Pressure: variable
- Heat: variable
- Class: thermal, regional

121

SEDIMENTARY ROCKS

BROKEN ROCK FRAGMENTS, seashells, and evaporites (minerals left behind by evaporation) are all materials that make up sedimentary rocks. These rocks form at the Earth's surface, in high mountains, deserts, and under the oceans. Geologists value sedimentary rocks because they provide an accurate record of the Earth's history.

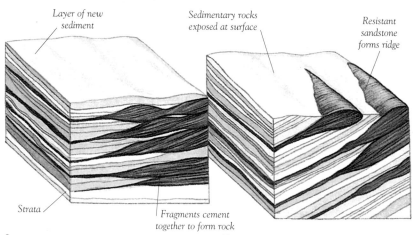

Layer of new sediment

Sedimentary rocks exposed at surface

Resistant sandstone forms ridge

Strata

Fragments cement together to form rock

LAYERS OF SEDIMENTS

Many sedimentary rocks are made up of fragments of other rocks. Agents such as wind, water, and ice deposit these fragments in layers called strata. More layers form, squashing the lower layers. Eventually, water-borne minerals cement the fragments together to form true rock.

ERODED ROCKS

Over time, buried rocks rise to the surface as the rocks above them erode away. Eroded rocks often form new rocks elsewhere. Some sedimentary rocks, such as sandstone, are more hard-wearing than others. When they reach the surface, they form distinct features, such as ridges.

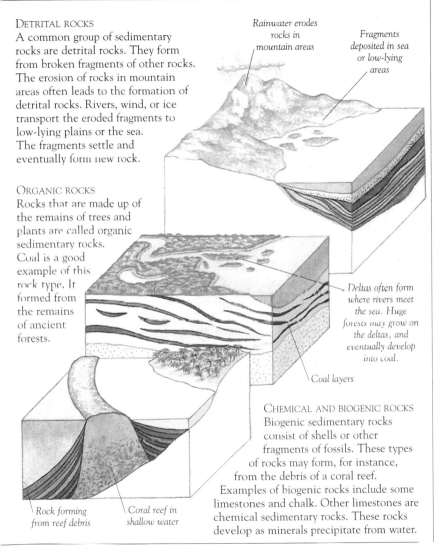

DETRITAL ROCKS

A common group of sedimentary rocks are detrital rocks. They form from broken fragments of other rocks. The erosion of rocks in mountain areas often leads to the formation of detrital rocks. Rivers, wind, or ice transport the eroded fragments to low-lying plains or the sea. The fragments settle and eventually form new rock.

ORGANIC ROCKS

Rocks that are made up of the remains of trees and plants are called organic sedimentary rocks. Coal is a good example of this rock type. It formed from the remains of ancient forests.

Rainwater erodes rocks in mountain areas

Fragments deposited in sea or low-lying areas

Deltas often form where rivers meet the sea. Huge forests may grow on the deltas, and eventually develop into coal.

Coal layers

Rock forming from reef debris

Coral reef in shallow water

CHEMICAL AND BIOGENIC ROCKS

Biogenic sedimentary rocks consist of shells or other fragments of fossils. These types of rocks may form, for instance, from the debris of a coral reef. Examples of biogenic rocks include some limestones and chalk. Other limestones are chemical sedimentary rocks. These rocks develop as minerals precipitate from water.

CONGLOMERATE AND BRECCIA

PEBBLES AND LARGER blocks that become cemented together form conglomerate and breccia. The difference between these two rocks is the roundness of the pebbles, or clasts. Conglomerate has rounded clasts. By contrast, breccia has angular clasts.

FLINT CONGLOMERATE
Conglomerates may consist of many types of clast, or only one. This example, called puddingstone, has only flint clasts. Flint is a tough material that often occurs in sedimentary rocks.

Wooden handle

Rounded flint clasts

HARD ROCK
Conglomerate can be a very hard-wearing rock. Its hardness proved useful in this Roman corngrinder, which consists of two blocks of conglomerate and a wooden handle. The grain was crushed between the two blocks of rock.

CONGLOMERATE FACTS

- Origin: marine, freshwater, and continental
- Grain size: very coarse
- Grain shape: round
- Fossils: very rare
- Class: detrital

BRECCIA
Most breccias form in mountain
areas, where the action of
the Sun's heat and ice
breaks rocks into
coarse, sharp-edged
clasts. This breccia
contains clasts of
different sizes, which
are bound together
by fine-grained
sediments.

LIMESTONE BRECCIA
Clasts of igneous,
metamorphic, and
sedimentary origin
occur in breccia.
The large, angular
fragments in this
example are limestone.
They are bound together
by a light-colored
"cement" that
is rich in calcite.

*Dark
fragments of
limestone*

MELTING GLACIER
Mountains produce vast
amounts of sediment as they
erode. Much of this sediment
gathers at the toes (ends) of
glaciers, which are the most
powerful eroders of mountains.
The debris at the toe of this
glacier in Alaska may
eventually form breccia.

SANDSTONE

MENTION THE WORD sand and many people will think of deserts and beaches. They may also think of sandstone, a sedimentary rock that is made of grains of sand. Sandstone forms in a range of environments and is often used as a building stone.

GRAINS IN SANDSTONE

Geologists define sandstone as a sedimentary rock that has grains between 0.02 and 2 mm in diameter. The grains are usually made of quartz, the most common mineral in sandstone.

Desert sand may one day form rock

Layers of medium grains

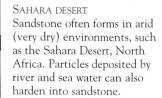

SAHARA DESERT

Sandstone often forms in arid (very dry) environments, such as the Sahara Desert, North Africa. Particles deposited by river and sea water can also harden into sandstone.

CARCASSONNE
Sandstone is a valuable building stone because it carves easily and resists weathering and pollution. The fortress city of Carcassonne, France, is largely built of this rock.

SANDSTONE FACTS

- Origin: marine, freshwater, and continental
- Grain size: medium
- Grain shape: angular, rounded
- Fossils: common
- Class: detrital

MILLET-SEED SANDSTONE
Grains of sand become rounded and polished in desert regions by the action of the wind. Eventually, the grains gather in layers that harden to form millet-seed sandstone. The dominant mineral in this example is quartz, but other minerals and rock fragments may be present.

Rounded grains characterize millet-seed sandstone

QUARTZ GRITSTONE
The sand grains in gritstone are more angular than those in millet-seed sandstone. Quartz makes up 75 percent of this rock, which can form on land or in water. Gritstones often contain fossils, particularly if the rock consists of particles that were laid down in the sea.

Angular-grained gritstone forms on land and in water

127

LIMESTONE

THE REMAINS OF ANCIENT creatures make up many types of limestone. Other varieties form when minerals precipitate out of water. All limestones, however, form where water is present and consist mainly of calcite. The main uses of limestone include building stone, cement, and fertilizers.

Tiny, rounded ooliths

OOLITIC LIMESTONE
Like most limestones, oolitic limestone forms in seawater. Tiny, round balls called ooliths give this rock its name. Ooliths develop in warm, shallow seas when calcite precipitates on fragments of bone and shell. They grow as they roll back and forth in the waves.

LIMESTONE FACTS

- Origin: marine or freshwater
- Grain size: coarse to fine
- Grain shape: angular, rounded
- Fossils: common
- Class: chemical, biogenic

Coral colony preserved as limestone

CORAL LIMESTONE
The fossilized remains of coral make up this variety of limestone. Millions of years in the future, today's living corals, such as the Great Barrier Reef, Australia, may develop into rock.

FRESHWATER LIMESTONE

Limestones are often rich in fossils, which give geologists precise information about the way in which the rock formed. This example contains the fossils of freshwater creatures, known as gastropods. They lived on the bed of an inland lake.

Shells bound together by fine-grained sediments

STONE FOREST

Limestone dissolves in rainwater, often creating spectacular landscapes. The stone forest of Kunming, China, is a fine example of eroded limestone.

Grains too small to see with a naked eye

CHALK

The skeletons of millions of tiny sea animals make up chalk, a very pure form of marine limestone. The grains in chalk are usually too small to see without a magnifying glass.

BUILDING BLOCKS

Limestone is often used to make cement. This house in Yemen, however, is built only from limestone blocks, with nothing binding them together.

COAL AND OIL

ROCKS ARE THE SOURCE of much of the world's energy. Coal is a sedimentary rock made from the plants and

COAL-POWERED STEAMSHIP

trees that covered the Earth millions of years ago. Oil is the remains of microscopic marine plants and animals. It is often found deep below the ground in sedimentary rocks. Geologists use their knowledge of rocks to help track down reserves of these valuable energy resources.

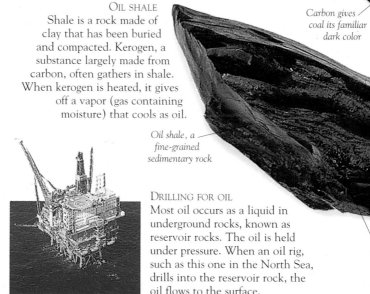

OIL SHALE
Shale is a rock made of clay that has been buried and compacted. Kerogen, a substance largely made from carbon, often gathers in shale. When kerogen is heated, it gives off a vapor (gas containing moisture) that cools as oil.

Carbon gives coal its familiar dark color

Oil shale, a fine-grained sedimentary rock

DRILLING FOR OIL
Most oil occurs as a liquid in underground rocks, known as reservoir rocks. The oil is held under pressure. When an oil rig, such as this one in the North Sea, drills into the reservoir rock, the oil flows to the surface.

Kerogen gathers in oil shale

Coal breaks easily into layers or blocks

BITUMINOUS COAL

The plants and trees of the ancient forest swamps are preserved in coal. Water preserved the vegetation, which gradually turned into bituminous, or household, coal. This hard, brittle rock is made up of about 60 percent carbon. When it burns, the other substances in coal form ash.

COAL-FORMING PROCESS

Plants and trees are the raw materials of coal. Peat forms as layers of these dead plants become compacted. Compressed peat then becomes lignite, a low-quality brown coal. Further pressure turns lignite into bituminous coal, which is refined into high-quality anthracite under yet more pressure and heat.

LAYERS OF WOODY PLANTS

COMPACTED LAYER OF PEAT

LIGNITE (30 PERCENT CARBON CONTENT)

BITUMINOUS COAL (60 PERCENT CARBON CONTENT)

ANTHRACITE (OVER 90 PERCENT CARBON CONTENT)

COAL FACTS

- Origin: continental
- Grain size: medium to fine
- Grain shape: none
- Fossils: common
- Class: chemical, organic

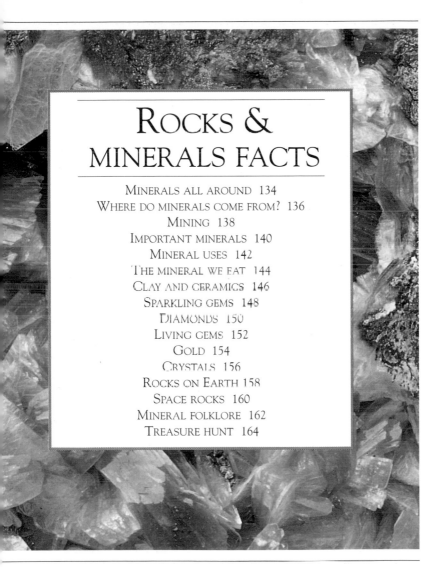

ROCKS &
MINERALS FACTS

MINERALS ALL AROUND

Minerals are naturally formed, inorganic substances that make up 99 percent of the Earth's crust. They usually contain metals joined with other elements (chemical substances.) Many are valuable and are the source of materials we use every day.

MINERAL	USEFUL COMPONENT	USED IN
Gibbsite	Aluminum	Pots and pans
Chromite	Chromium	Stainless-steel sinks
Chalcopyrite	Copper	Electrical wiring
Magnetite	Iron	Frying pans
Galena	Lead	Car batteries
Silver	Native metal	Cutlery
Gold	Native metal	Jewelry
Cassiterite	Tin	Paint cans
Sylvite	Potash	Fertilizers
Sphalerite	Zinc	Brass bed frames
Cinnabar	Mercury	Thermometers
Wolframite	Tungsten	Lightbulbs
Calcite	Calcium	Toothpaste

MINERALS IN SPACE

Minerals are the most common materials in the Earth's crust. They are also found in rocks on the Moon and on rocky planets such as Mars, Venus, and Mercury. Even asteroids are made of minerals. Future generations may use the metals and minerals on asteroids as the raw materials for building structures in space.

The planet Mercury has mineral deposits from volcanic eruptions.

MINERALS IN THE WILD

- All rocks are made of one or more minerals.

- Minerals are everywhere underfoot. Even soil is littered with tiny, ground-up particles of them.

- We know of about 3,500 minerals. Each year, 20 or so new types are discovered.

- Only about 100 minerals are common. The rest are rare – many are rarer than gold.

- The most common minerals of all are silicates (compounds of silicon and oxygen), which make up 93% of the rocks in the world. There are about 1,000 minerals in the silicate family.

MINERAL CONSUMERS

The following most-used metals are all found in minerals. The table shows the amount used in a lifetime by the average person living in the United States:

METAL	AMOUNT USED
Aluminum	3,593 lbs (1,633 kg)
Copper	1,496 lbs (680 kg)
Iron	32,699 lbs (14,863 kg)
Lead	803 lbs (365 kg)
Zinc	748 lbs (340 kg)

The tail of a comet (a chunk of rock and ice left over from the beginning of the Solar System)

OUT OF THIS WORLD

Meteorites are space rocks that land on Earth. They are the remains of larger objects, such as comets, that have broken up in the Earth's atmosphere. Meteorites mostly contain iron and stony minerals, but they also contain very small diamonds. About three percent of the carbon in meteorites is pure diamond. Sadly, it doesn't mean that finding a meteorite will make you rich. The diamonds, known as nanodiamonds, are tiny. They are no bigger than a hundred millionths of an inch and are invisible to the human eye.

WHERE DO MINERALS COME FROM?

Minerals are found all over the world. Certain parts of the world are rich in minerals because of the elements that exist beneath the Earth's surface. Here are the most important sources of some well-known minerals.

ALUMINUM
Bauxite, the rock from which most aluminum comes, is mostly mined in Brazil and Australia.

ANTIMONY
The leading miners of antimony are China, Bolivia, and South Africa.

COPPER
The two biggest miners of copper ore are Chile and the US.

CHROMIUM
This mineral is mined primarily in Turkey, Kazakhstan, and South Africa.

EMERALD
The biggest emeralds are found in black limestone mines in Colombia.

GOLD
South Africa has the largest number of gold mines.

IRON
Russia, Brazil, Australia, and China are the main sources of iron.

LEAD
The principal countries mining lead are China, Australia, and the US.

MANGANESE
This mineral is found in South Africa, Gabon, and Brazil.

NICKEL
Russia, Canada, and Australia are the main sources of nickel.

PHOSPHATE
The biggest producers of phosphate rock are China and the US.

SILVER
The biggest silver mines are in Mexico, the US, and Peru.

TIN
The largest tin mines are in China, Peru, and Indonesia.

TURQUOISE
Iran has mined turquoise since about 1300 A.D.

URANIUM
The leading source of uranium is Canada.

ZINC
The biggest miners of zinc are Australia, Canada, and China.

NATIVE METALS

A metal that is found in the ground in a pure form is a native metal. Nuggets or flakes of a native mineral can be taken straight from the rocks because they are not mixed up with other substances.

COMMON	RARE
Copper	Iron
Gold	Lead
Platinum	Mercury
Silver	Palladium
	Tin
	Zinc

The native metal, zinc

COMPOUND ORES

Most metals are found in the ground joined to elements such as sulphur, oxygen, or carbon. They are called compound ores. Here are some common metals that can be found in compound ores.

SULFIDES	OXIDES	CARBONATES
Copper	Iron	Copper
Lead	Aluminum	Lead
Mercury	Tin	Iron
Nickel	Titanium	Manganese
Silver	Magnesium	Zinc

FLAME TEST

To find out what is in a mineral, geologists use an easy lab test. They dip a length of platinum wire into the powdered mineral. Then they hold it into a flame to discover which metal it contains.

COLOR OF FLAME	METAL
Steady yellow	Sodium
Orange-red	Calcium
Bright green	Copper
Steady yellow-green	Barium
Spurting bright red	Strontium
Vermilion-red	Lithium
Violet	Potassium

MOST COMMON METALS

The most common metals in the Earth's crust are:

- Aluminum
- Potassium
- Iron
- Calcium
- Sodium
- Magnesium

A cross-section that shows mining of the Earth's crust, which has a depth of up to 43 miles (70 km).

CRUST

The deepest hole reaches 7.5 miles (12 km).

MANTLE

MINING

MINING FOR MINERALS

There are many ways to mine rocks and minerals. The chosen method depends on where the ore (the rock holding the mineral) lies. Some ores are near the surface. Others are deep underground.

- The earliest mines were dug about 8,000 years ago. They were small pits and tunnels used to find flint, a rock. Early people used flint to make tools or spearheads and arrowheads.

*Stone Age
flint arrowhead*

- The first mines for metal were dug about 5,500 years ago. The metals, tin and copper ore, were crushed and heated together to make bronze.

- The deepest mines are the gold mines of South Africa, although even these only scratch the Earth's crust. The record holder is Western Deep Mine. Some of its tunnels are 2.2 miles (3.5 km) down, and are now being extended to 2.5 miles (4 km).

- Not all mines are holes in the ground. Along the coast of Namibia, Africa, large ships vacuum up sand from the sea bottom and sift it for diamonds.

MINING UNDERGROUND

- If ore lies in vertical shafts, miners slice the ore into horizontal sections and dig upward. When they have dug out a section, they fill the space with waste to make a platform. From there they can mine the slice above. This is called cut and fill mining.

- Room and pillar mining is used if the ore lies in a horizontal bed. Miners dig out the ore but leave some as pillars to hold up the rocks above. Coal and uranium are often mined in this way.

MINING NEAR THE SURFACE

- Where mineral-rich gravel lies in thick beds, a floating dredge uses a chain of buckets to scoop up the ore. This is called dredging.

- Open-cast mining involves blasting beds of ore along ledges of an open pit.

- Placer mining is a way of mining metals from gravel and sand by washing them out with fast-flowing water.

- Quarrying is a way of cutting, drilling, or blasting minerals, such as marble, that lie at the surface.

TOP TEN MINERALS MINED WORLDWIDE

An ore is a mineral with enough metal inside it to be worth mining. Only about 100 ores are considered rich enough to be mined. The rest are not worth the expense of extraction.

MINERAL AND USES	AMOUNT MINED IN THE YEAR 2000
Iron ore (for steel)	919 million tons (938 million tonnes)
Phosphates (for agricultural fertilizers)	136 million tons (139 million tonnes)
Bauxite (for aluminum)	124 million tons (127 million tonnes)
Chromite (for stainless steel)	13.4 million tons (13.7 million tonnes)
Copper (for electrical goods)	12.6 million tons (12.9 million tonnes)
Zinc (for brass)	8.5 million tons (8.7 million tonnes)
Manganese (for steel)	7.4 million tons (7.5 million tonnes)
Titanium (for paints and pigments)	5.7 million tons (5.8 million tonnes)
Lead (for car batteries)	2.9 million tons (3.0 million tonnes)
Nickel (for stainless steel and batteries)	1.1 million tons (1.2 million tonnes)

Open-cast mining for gold and silver at Martha Mine, in Waihi, New Zealand

IMPORTANT MINERALS

HOW MINERALS ARE MADE

- Diamonds form 75–120 miles (120–190 km) deep within the Earth's crust, when searing heat and pressure turn pure carbon into diamond crystals.

- Volcanoes bring diamond crystals toward the surface, and deposit them in rock called kimberlite.

- Crystals of quartz form after silicon and oxygen brew together in hot water deep in the Earth's crust. The crystals are tiny, but grow to fill the spaces around them.

- Copper forms in confined spaces such as between two beds of rock, where it grows in thin sheets. The branch-like form it develops is described as "dendritic," from the Greek word, *dendron*, meaning tree.

- Galena, the main ore from which lead is obtained, forms when hot fluids seep up through the Earth's crust and minerals crystalize from them.

- Opals were made millions of years ago when receding sea water deposited silica-rich solutions in rock cavities.

- Feldspar is one of the most common minerals. This silicate forms when molten magma underground, or lava on the surface, cools and turns to rock.

- Stalactites and stalagmites are formed on the ceilings and floors of caves by calcite-rich water dripping and leaving a deposit. It gradually builds up over time. They grow less than an inch each year.

LUCKY FIND

In the 1980s, miners digging for tourmaline gemstones in Namibia, Africa, came across a great gap in the rocks, lined with crystals of quartz. One six-sided monster weighed 1,300 lbs (590 kg). Others were even bigger. The crystals grew to giant sizes due to cracks in the rock.

Purple tourmaline crystal and clear quartz crystal

MINERALS WE CANNOT DO WITHOUT

- Aluminum is the most abundant metal found in minerals. It is used in cans and in building construction.

- Antimony is a metal used to harden lead in batteries and cables, make fireworks, and in glassmaking.

- Chromium is used to harden steel and make machine tools, kitchen utensils, and ball bearings.

- Copper is used in electric wires and cables. It is also used in plumbing and building, to make alloys (mixtures of metals) like brass and bronze, and in cooking utensils.

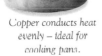

Copper conducts heat evenly – ideal for cooking pans.

- Feldspar is the most common mineral and is used to make glass and ceramics. It is also used in soaps, abrasives, cement, and concrete.

- Fluorspar is a mineral used to make hydrofluoric acid for pottery. It is also used to produce toothpaste and paint.

- Iron, a metal found in minerals, is used to make steel, magnets, auto parts, and catalysts.

- Lead, another metal found in minerals, is used to make batteries, solders, seals, TV tubes, and ballast.

- Limestone is a rock made mostly of the mineral calcite. It is used as a building stone, and to make cement. It is also used to make paper, plastics, and glass, and to smelt iron ore.

- Manganese is essential for making iron and steel, and is also used in alloys, batteries, and dyes.

- Mica is a group of important minerals, which are used in paints, plastics, roofing, and rubber.

- Nickel is a metal used in an alloy to make stainless steel, and in the chemical industry as a catalyst. It is also used in the catalytic converters of cars, and to make jewelry.

- Silver is used to make jewelry and coins. It is also used in photography, and in some electrical equipment.

- Titanium is a metal found in minerals, and is used in jet engines, aircraft frames, missile parts, and machinery.

Titanium is used in aircraft parts, such as this Rolls Royce turbofan, because it is so lightweight and strong.

141

MINERAL USES

A FAMILY CAR

Iron and steel*	2,124 lbs (965 kg)
Plastics (not a mineral)	250 lbs (114 kg)
Aluminum*	240 lbs (109 kg)
Rubber (not a mineral)	140 lbs (64 kg)
Sand (a mix of minerals)	89 lbs (40 kg)
Carbon*	50 lbs (23 kg)
Copper	41 lbs (19 kg)
Silicon*	41 lbs (19 kg)
Lead*	24 lbs (11 kg)
Zinc*	22 lbs (10 kg)
Manganese*	17 lbs (8 kg)
Chromium*	15 lbs (7 kg)
Nickel*	9 lbs (4 kg)
Magnesium*	4.5 lbs (2 kg)
Sulfur	2 lbs (0.9 kg)

Plus traces of antimony, barium*, cadmium*, fluorspar, gallium*, graphite, halite, mica, nitrogen*, potash, tin*, titanium*

Key: * These materials are elements found in minerals, rather than minerals in their own right.

There is no lead in pencil lead. Graphite is used instead, but it is a soft mineral and needs to be supported by the surrounding wood.

A LIGHTBULB

- Base (to fit into a lamp): aluminum* or brass* (zinc and copper)

- Fuse (to protect the circuit): nickel*, manganese*, copper alloys

- Stem wires (to hold the filament up): nickel-iron alloy* and a copper sleeve

- Support wires (to help keep filament in place): molybdenum*

- Filament (to glow as current flows through it: tungsten*

- Heat deflector (to protect neck of bulb): aluminum*

- Bulb (glass to seal all the insides): silica*, soda ash*, lime*, coal*, and salt*

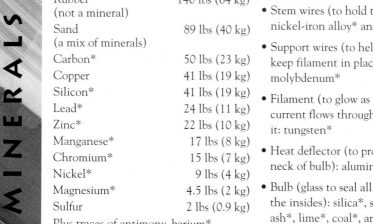

A PENCIL

- Lead (to write with): graphite and clay

- Eraser (for rubbing out): sulfur, calcium, barium, and pumice to strengthen the rubber gum

- Metal band (to hold the rubber in place): aluminum

- Paint (to color the wood): several minerals depending on the color

A TUBE OF TOOTHPASTE

TOOTHPASTE COMPONENTS	MINERALS USED
Abrasives (to rub away food bits and plaque):	Minerals such as aluminum oxide, limestone, phosphate, and silica
Whitener (to make the toothpaste look bright and fresh):	Titanium dioxide, from minerals such as rutile and ilmentite (ores of titanium)
Protection against cavities (to stop tooth decay):	Fluoride, from the mineral fluorite

WHO INVENTED CONCRETE?

The ancient Romans knew how to make concrete. They used lime and volcanic ash in their cement mix. The result was a concrete so strong that many of their bridges, roads, and buildings still survive. After Rome fell (A.D. 476), the skill of making cement was forgotten – until British engineer, John Smeaton, rediscovered it in 1756. He developed a mix using hydraulic lime that hardens in water and used it to rebuild Eddystone lighthouse in Cornwall, England.

CONCRETE

- Cement (the gray powder that makes concrete go hard): limestone 60%, silica 25%, alumina 5%, gypsum, iron oxide 10%

- Sand (small particles of rocks and minerals up to 0.04 inches (2 mm) wide): several minerals including quartz, feldspar, calcite, and silica

- Coarse aggregate (gravel, crushed rocks): many common silicate minerals, such as quartz and feldspar

- Water: not a mineral

The drum on a concrete mixer revolves to prevent the mix from setting.

THE MINERAL WE EAT

WHAT IS SALT?

- Salt is a mineral and a crystal. The crystals look like tiny, glass sugar cubes. They appear to be white because they reflect light. Impurities in salt can also make it look gray, yellow, or even red.

- Salt's mineral name is halite.

- Salt is made from two elements, sodium and chlorine. Each is lethal if large quantities are absorbed on their own, but together they provide humans and animals with an essential mineral.

- Our bodies need small amounts of salt in order to work properly. Salt helps the flow of water between blood and cells. It also plays a part in the movements of muscles. The average adult body contains about 7 ounces (170 grams) of salt.

SALTY PAST

- In ancient times, salt was so rare and valuable in some regions that it was traded for the same amount in gold.

- The African salt trade has existed for over a thousand years, with traders traveling hundreds of miles. In a long camel caravan, each animal might be carrying 550 lbs (250 kg) of salt.

- The main highway of ancient Rome was the *Via Salacia* – the Salt Road. It was used to carry salt from the Tiber River, where barges brought it from saltpans by the sea.

- Roman soldiers were paid a *salarium* (from which we get the word "salary"). This was the money used to pay for their salt ration.

HOW SALT IS USED

- Salt is spread on roads in winter to melt the ice (it lowers the melting point of ice) and thus clear a safe path for drivers.

- In the chemical industry, salt is used to make soda (which in turn goes into making soap and glass).

- Salt is used to make ceramic glazes, textile dyes, and water softeners. It also helps to treat sewage.

- Only a small amount of salt ends up being used as seasoning in food.

Statue of a salt worker from Portugal spreading salt

GETTING SALT

- Sea salt comes from the sea. Seawater is about 3.5% salt and other minerals. The sun evaporates seawater penned in large shallow ponds to leave salt that is 95–98% pure. Most sea salt comes from China, France, and India.

Rock salt is used for homeopathic remedies.

- Salt that lies underground is known as rock salt. It formed millions of years ago when seas evaporated. It can be extracted by sinking shafts and digging great corridors of salt through the rock.

Sea salt is often used as a seasoning in food.

- Some rock salt is gathered by drilling. Twin pipes are drilled into a known salt deposit. The inner pipe pumps freshwater into the deposit that dissolves the salt into brine. The outer pipe sucks the brine back to the surface, where it evaporates in enclosed vessels called vacuum pans, leaving just the salt.

OLD SALT MINES

- The Hallstatt salt mine in Austria is one of the oldest salt mines in the world. People have been mining deposits here since the Iron Age (c. 1000 B.C.). Over the centuries, more than 25 miles (40 km) of galleries have been dug.

- The Wieliczka salt mine in Poland has been mined since the 13th century and has over 186 miles (300 km) of galleries with salt statues and artworks.

- About 1,600 years ago, the Chinese drilled into the ground with bamboo pipes to bring salty brine to the surface.

HOW MUCH?

In all, about 210 million tons (214 million tonnes) of salt a year are produced. Just seven countries produce more than half of it.

COUNTRY	AMOUNT PRODUCED IN A YEAR
U.S.A.	44 million tons
China	31 million tons
Germany	15.5 million tons
Canada	12.3 million tons
India	14.2 million tons
Mexico	8.4 million tons
Australia	7.8 million tons

CLAY AND CERAMICS

WHAT IS CLAY?

An Ancient Roman clay jug, used to store wine.

- Clay is a type of sedimentary rock.

- It takes a microscope to see the tiny crystals of alumina and silica that make up clay. They are less than a hundred millionths of an inch in size.

- The color of clay comes from other materials in it. If it is gray, then it contains carbon (plant material). If red, there are iron oxides in it.

- There are two main kinds of clay, expandable and nonexpandable. The first can absorb so much water that it turns liquid. The second softens in water but never turns into slush. These clays can be baked to harden them, after which they cannot be softened by water.

TYPES OF CLAY

- China clay, called kaolin, is a pure white clay that makes the finest pottery. It is also used in textiles to give weight to the fabric, and in paper making to give paper a gloss.

- Ball clay is not as pure as kaolin, but it is much easier to mold into shapes. It has a dark brown or blackish color, and is used to make ceramics.

- Fire clay resists heat well, so it is used to make the firebricks lining the insides of furnaces, kilns, and fireplaces.

- Earthenware clay is the most common clay. It has iron impurities that make it harden at lower temperatures than other clays. It is the most common clay for making pottery.

- Bentonite clay is used in oil exploration as a drilling mud because it is so slippery and provides lubrication for the drill.

A modern Pynaker Delft porcelain jar

FIRING CLAY

When clay is heated to very high temperatures in a kiln (when making pottery or bricks), it goes through a chemical change. Water is driven off and tiny grains of silica fuse together. The clay changes into a new mineral called mullite that is glassy and hard. China clay is fired at a higher temperature than common clay. The porcelain that results has a far finer finish than other pottery.

Ancient Egyptian pottery kiln

EATING CLAY

- Wild macaws often peck at clay on riverbanks. It helps them to digest the poisons in some of the seeds they eat.

- Elephants lick clay from mud holes to help digest leaves they have eaten during the day.

- Mountain gorillas in Rwanda, Africa, eat clay that resembles kaolinite. It lines their gut, and treats stomach upsets.

- Kaolinite is the main ingredient in many tonics that are sold for human digestive problems.

OTHER USES OF CLAY

- Clay is used to make ceramic tiles, pottery, porcelain, baths, sinks, bricks, drainpipes, and also firebricks for chimneys and furnaces.

- It keeps soil fertile from year to year, although too much clay in soil will make it heavy and will stop air and water from getting in.

- Clay also helps soil to retain the fertilizer it obtains from manure.

- It helps plants to grow by absorbing ammonia and other gases.

- Fuller's earth is a clay material used to purify fats and vegetable oils.

MINING CLAY

- China clay is mined by water washing it from the ground. Jets of water are used to blast the clay loose.

- Then a thick sludge of clay and water is piped away to vats where grit, such as sand and mica, is washed out.

- The brightness of the clay is improved by bleaching it and using other methods to remove iron, titanium, and unwanted materials.

- Finally, the clay is filtered and dried. It may be packed into cakes, or into sacks, or else shipped still wet to paper mills.

SPARKLING GEMS

WHAT IS A GEM?

- A gemstone is any mineral or stone that people can cut and polish for jewelry or ornaments, and has a beautiful color.

- A gemstone must also be durable – hard enough to survive constant use, and it must be rare.

- Although marble looks beautiful once it is polished, it is not a gemstone. It is not rare and is too easily damaged to be long-lasting.

- In the wild, gemstones are rough and dull. They only give off sparkle and fire after they have been carefully cut and turned into gems.

- Out of over 3,500 minerals, only about 50 are commonly cut as gems.

- Precious gemstones are those that are used in jewelry and have great value.

BEAUTIFUL COLORS

Tiny amounts of metal within a gemstone give it a beautiful hue.

- The metal chromium gives rubies their deep reds, and turns emeralds and garnets a brilliant green.

Brilliant-cut green garnet

- Iron makes garnets and sapphires glow with tints of red, blue, green, or yellow.

Polished green malachite

- Copper brings blues and greens to turquoise and malachite.

- The manganese in garnet and rhodonite adds a blush of pink or orange.

Oval pink rhodonite with manganese deposits

PRECIOUS OR NOT?

Only seven gemstones are said to be precious:

- Diamond
- Ruby
- Sapphire
- Emerald
- Aquamarine
- Topaz
- Opal

Brilliant-cut aquamarine

HOW DO GEMS FORM?

NAME OF GEM	WHERE IT IS FORMED
Emerald	This precious gem is formed deep down in the Earth's crust when hot molten granite reacts with chromium rocks.
Garnet	This semi-precious gem is found in metamorphic rocks where heat and pressure have altered existing rocks.
Jade	Jade is created in the crust and carried to the surface when mountain ranges, such as the Himalayas, are thrust up.
Turquoise	One of the first gemstones to be mined, turquoise is deposited by surface water flowing through cracks in aluminum-rich rocks.
Zircon	This gem is formed in reactions deep in the Earth's crust between molten granite and shale and limestone.

Brilliant-cut zircon

FAKE GEMS

Gems are so valuable that, for thousands of years, people have made fake copies of them.

- Glass is used as a fake gem because it can take any color or shape. The giveaway is if it has tiny bubbles within, or a swirly texture.

- Compared to real gems, glass ones are soft and easily chipped or scratched.

WHERE ARE GEMS FOUND?

- In the wild, gems are rare. A rich diamond mine may sort through 98 tons (100 tonnes) of waste rock to find just 25 carats of diamonds – that is about 0.2 ounces (5 grams), or a sugar cube.

- The best sapphires come from Sri Lanka and Australia.

- The finest red rubies come from Burma, although more are mined in nearby Thailand.

Cut rubies

DIAMONDS

FAMOUS DIAMONDS

- In 1905, the biggest diamond the world has ever seen was found in South Africa. Called the Cullinan Diamond, it weighed 3,106 carats. It was cut into nine big stones and 96 smaller ones.

- The Excelsior, another giant from South Africa, weighed 995 carats when discovered in 1893. Since then, it has been cut into 21 gleaming gems.

- The Hope Diamond is said to bring bad luck. Louis XVI of France (1754–1793) once owned this indigo blue beauty – and he was beheaded. Today, the diamond is held in the Smithsonian Institution in Washington, D.C.

- Mogul rulers of India once owned the Koh-i-Noor Diamond. In 1526, its value was claimed to be as much as all the world's shopping for a single day. Today, the Koh-i-Noor is part of the British crown jewels.

- The third largest diamond ever seen in the world is the Great Mogul. It was owned by Shah Jehan, who built the Taj Mahal in India. It was discovered in the 1600s, but has since disappeared. It may have been cut up into many smaller stones.

- Today, the biggest cut diamond in the world is the Star of Africa. It weighs 530 carats and sits in the Royal Scepter, part of the crown jewels of Britain.

- The Star of Sierra Leone is one of the biggest rough (uncut) diamonds in the world. It was found in Sierra Leone, Africa, in 1972, and weighs 969 carats.

CUT DIAMONDS

- There are many ways to shape diamonds, but most of them are cut as brilliants.
- A brilliant stone has 58 polished flat faces (facets) to bring out its sparkle. The angles of the facets are worked out mathematically.
- Only another diamond is hard enough and sharp enough to shape a new diamond.

Rough diamond with convex crystal faces

PRICELESS DIAMONDS

- The most expensive diamond ever sold was a pear-shaped, 100-carat diamond, sold for $16.5 million in 1995. The buyer was the owner of a chain of jewelry shops in Saudi Arabia.

- In 1980, a single pair of diamond earrings was sold at an auction for $7.2 million – the most expensive diamond earrings ever.

- In 1074, the Queen of Hungary's crown was decorated with uncut diamonds – this Holy Crown of Hungary is the oldest known piece of diamond jewelry.

- The most precious gem in the world is the Hope Diamond, recently valued at a quarter of a billion dollars.

Brilliant-cut diamond

DIAMONDS ARE FOREVER

- In India, people have mined diamonds from sand and gravel riverbeds for about 2,800 years. Until the 1700s, most of the world's diamonds came from here.

- Since then, big deposits have been found in Brazil (1700s), in South Africa (1860s), in Siberia (1950s), and most recently in western Canada.

- Diamonds really do last forever. The Hope Diamond, for example, is thought to be over a billion years old.

- About 20 percent of all diamonds go into jewelry. The rest make cutting and polishing tools and laboratory instruments.

DIAMOND LOVE

- In 1477, Archduke Maximilian of Austria gave a diamond ring to Mary of Burgundy for their engagement. The tradition continues today.

- Most women wear diamond engagement rings on the third finger of the left hand. This stems from the Ancient Egyptian belief that the "vein of love" ran straight from this finger to the heart.

- In the 1500s, lovers in England scratched romantic vows on windows with their diamond rings. They were called scribbling rings.

Ring with a cluster of diamonds held in a claw setting

151

ROCKS & MINERAL FACTS

ALIVE AND PRECIOUS

All gemstones come from rocks –
except for four. These exceptions to
the rule all come from some form of
living thing.

- Amber: the sap of pine trees
- Coral: tiny sea-dwelling animals
- Jet: ancient forests and swamps
- Pearl: oysters and other mollusks

JET

Jet is a form of coal that can be polished
to look like black glass.

- Jet forms when wood rots in stagnant
  water and then is buried deep
  underground. Here it is squeezed and
  heated until it turns into a form of coal.

- Jet has a deep black color. It is fairly
  soft, and easy to turn into ornaments,
  buttons, and jewelry.

- Over 2,000 years ago, Britons mined
  jet and shipped it across the Roman
  empire for use in jewelry.

- Jet was a popular gem in the 1800s,
  and was widely used
  as jewelry for
  mourning.

*Rose carved in
jet from the late
19th century*

AMBER

This gem comes from the resin, or sap,
of ancient pine trees.
After the sap was
buried in the
ground, it turned
into a mineral.

- Today, amber
  is either
  gathered on
  the seashore
  or mined from
  the ground.

*Spider
trapped
in amber*

- Amber is mostly transparent.

- It ranges in color from light yellow to
  dark golden brown, although it may
  have hues of orange, red, or white.

- Some pieces of amber are cloudy due
  to the air trapped inside.

- Sometimes insects and pieces of moss
  are trapped in amber because it was
  soft and sticky when it was fresh sap.

- The main source of amber is the
  southeastern coast of the Baltic Sea.

- Amber is relatively soft, so it is easy to
  carve into ornaments.

- When amber is made into beads or
  other jewelry, it is polished until
  it glows.

CORAL

This gem comes from the skeletons of tiny sea animals that live in colonies. A coral polyp (as the animal is known) takes up calcium carbonate minerals from the sea and builds itself a hard limestone home. As one polyp dies, the next generation builds on top of it.

- The most valuable coral is red.

- The skeleton of corals is polished to bring out its beautiful red, pink, rose, or white colors.

- The best coral is made into beads or carved into figures.

Red coral from the Mediterranean Sea

PEARL

This gem grows inside any mollusk (shellfish) with a pearly lining. If a speck of grit becomes stuck inside its shell, the animal surrounds the object with layers of pearly nacre (aragonite). Over time, these layers form a pearl.

- Gem-quality pearls come from oysters that live in tropical seas. The best are perfectly round, but others may be egg- or pear-shaped.

- Pearls can be white, cream, light rose, gray, blue red, or violet.

- Freshwater pearls come from Europe and the US. Seawater pearls are harvested in the Persian Gulf and other warmwater locations.

- Large, perfectly round pearls are some of the most valuable gems.

CULTURED PEARLS

There are never enough natural pearls to go around, so people also cultivate them. In Japan, young oysters are placed in special beds. After growing for three years, their shells are opened and a tiny pellet of nacre is placed inside. Then the oysters are put into cages (to keep them safe) and lowered into the sea. One to three years later, the oyster shells are opened. Only one in 20 of them will have made a gem-quality pearl.

A string of cultured pearls

ROCKS & MINERALS FACTS

MEASURING GOLD

- An ounce of gold is heavier than an ounce of steel. That is because gold is measured in "troy weight" where ounces are heavier than in the "avoirdupois weight" commonly used to weigh other items.

- Pure gold is 24 carats (written as K). But a pure gold bracelet is so soft that it bends and scratches easily. So jewelry is often made of 18 K gold (18 parts gold and 6 parts of another metal) to make it hard wearing.

- From every 0.98 ton (1 tonne) of ore dug from a gold mine, only 1 oz (28 g) of gold is extracted.

- Gold nuggets are rare chunks of pure gold. They are usually found in the sand and gravel beds of streams.

- The biggest nugget ever was the Welcome Stranger found in Australia in 1869. It weighed 156 lb (70.9 kg).

- Seawater contains tiny amounts of gold, but they are so tiny that extraction would be too expensive.

Gold nugget

EVERYDAY GOLD

Gold has many uses. It is pure and easy to shape, it conducts electricity, and reflects heat and radiation well.

- Dentists worldwide use about 50 lbs (23 kg) a day to fill teeth. It takes 18,130 tons (18,500 tonnes) of ore to produce this much gold.

- There is a tiny amount of gold in the mouthpiece transmitter of most telephones.

- The chips in computer keyboards use gold circuits to pass messages round the computer.

The gold wires inside the computer chip connect to metal pins, which are then soldered to the circuit board.

- Car manufacturers use gold electrical contacts to trigger the airbag release in car accidents.

- The biggest telescopes in the world use pure gold to coat their secondary mirrors, which reflect the image to the eyepiece.

- The plastic visor of an astronaut's spacesuit helmet is coated with gold to protect the astronaut from the powerful rays of the sun.

Aztec cast-gold rattle,
(c A.D. 1100–1520)

OLD GOLD

- The people of ancient Mesopotamia (now Iraq) were making golden cups and jewelry over 5,500 years ago.

- For ancient Egyptians, gold was the metal of the gods, and belonged to their rulers, the pharaohs.

- Gold was first used as money in ancient Lydia (now Turkey) about 2,700 years ago. Small gold coins were minted with the king's head stamped onto them.

- Wealthy Aztecs in Mexico filled their burial tombs with gold objects for use in the afterlife.

- In the Middle Ages, (c A.D. 476–1450) alchemists hunted for chemical formulas to turn cheap and common metals into gold. They did not succeed.

WHERE DO WE GET IT?

Nugget of gold in quartz crystal

WHO MINES THE MOST GOLD?	HOW MUCH EACH YEAR
South Africa	512 tons (522 tonnes)
United States	322 tons (329 tonnes)
Australia	248 tons (253 tonnes)
Canada	135 tons (150 tonnes)
Russia	139 tons (142 tonnes)
China	133 tons (136 tonnes)

GOLD BARS

After gold is separated from rock ore, it is purified, then poured into molds and cast into small bars. These are easy to stack and transport. Each bar is about 99.99 percent pure. It takes about 980 tons (1,000 tonnes) of ore to produce a single bar of gold.

WHO BUYS IT?

COUNTRIES THAT BUY THE MOST GOLD	HOW MUCH DO THEY BUY EACH YEAR?
India	588 tons (600 tonnes)
United States	401 tons (409 tonnes)
European Union	367 tons (374 tonnes)
China	180 tons (184 tonnes)
Saudi Arabia	166 tons (169 tonnes)
Egypt	125 tons (128 tonnes)
Turkey	123 tons (126 tonnes)

CRYSTALS

WHAT IS A CRYSTAL?

- Crystals are solid minerals that have enough room underground to grow into regular geometric shapes.

- Crystals form when molten rock, deep in the Earth, cools and hardens. As the temperature drops, the atoms of the crystals come together into neat geometric shapes.

- Crystals also form when hot flowing liquids, deep underground, find their way into cracks and deposit dissolved minerals there.

- Most crystals take thousands of years to grow (although salt crystals can form in a few days).

- Minerals with atoms that grow into irregular shapes are called amorphous. Graphite is an example of an amorphous mineral.

HEALING CRYSTALS

For thousands of years, people have believed that crystals have special powers to help the sick or calm someone who is upset. Healing comes from wearing or holding the crystal close to the skin.

CRYSTAL	BENEFITS
Amazonite	Calms the mind
Amethyst	Cures acne
Blue-lace agate	Helps to cope with anger
Green calcite	Banishes fear
Hematite	Relieves the stress of air travel
Jade	Relaxation
Lapis lazuli	Promotes friendship
Onyx	Changes bad habits
Quartz crystals	Help to fend off headaches
Sapphire	Helps mental clarity
Yellow topaz	Reduces the misery of colds and flu

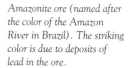

Amazonite ore (named after the color of the Amazon River in Brazil). The striking color is due to deposits of lead in the ore.

QUARTZ

- Quartz is one of the most common minerals on Earth.

- Quartz is also known as rock crystal, and is made almost entirely from atoms of silicon and oxygen. It is so hard that it cannot be scratched with a knife.

- Crystals of quartz are six-sided columns. In the right conditions, quartz crystals can grow to a giant size – up to 12 ft (4 m) long.

Smoky quartz

- Colored quartz has many names: violet is called amethyst, black is called smoky quartz, and yellow is known as citrine. The colors come from tiny impurities in the crystals, such as iron, carbon, or manganese.

- Opal is a mineral that is similar to quartz, but it contains water. When you hold an opal, the warmth of your hand heats the water and changes the color.

- A fortune teller's crystal ball is traditionally made of quartz.

- Quartz is used to make glass, paint, and abrasives. Its crystals are also used in heat-ray lamps, prisms, and in many kinds of electrical equipment.

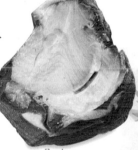

Opal

- The word crystal comes from the Greek word *kyros*, meaning "icy cold." The ancient Greeks once thought that quartz crystals were ice that had frozen so hard they would never melt.

Snowflakes are tiny water crystals.

SNOW CRYSTALS

Not all crystals are minerals. When water freezes, its molecules stack together in a regular way to form tiny, six-sided crystals. In a freezing cloud, ice crystals clump together to create big fluffy snowflakes. As each snowflake is blown about, it grows in slightly different conditions – that is why no two snowflakes are exactly alike.

157

ROCKS ON EARTH

ALL KINDS OF ROCK

- All rocks are a combination of two or more minerals. Granite, for example, is made of three minerals: quartz, feldspar, and mica.

- Rocks that are ores contain deposits of metal. Iron, aluminum, lead, tin, gold, and uranium are all extracted from ores.

- Some rocks float. Pumice is a kind of lava from volcanoes. When the gases within it escape, they leave behind thousands of tiny air holes. This makes this rock light enough to bob on water.

- Most rocks are hard and stiff, but some are bendy. A rare type of sandstone in India can be flexed back and forth by hand.

- If lightning strikes a beach, it sometimes melts the sand to form a glassy rock called fulgurite.

FAMOUS ROCK FORMATIONS

- The Rock of Gibraltar is a huge mass of limestone on the southern tip of Spain. It rises 1,398 ft (426 m) above the sea.

- Giant's Causeway in Northern Ireland is a collection of about 40,000 basalt pillars packed close together. It was made by a flow of cooling lava.

- Ayer's Rock in Australia is a giant outcrop of ancient sandstone that rises 1,100 ft (335 m) above the surrounding land.

- Delicate Arch, in Utah, is an arch of gracefully weathered sandstone. The opening in the middle is 45 ft (13.5 m) high and wide enough to drive trucks through. Nearby are hundreds of other rocky arches, all carved by the desert wind.

- Shiprock Pinnacle in New Mexico is a huge pillar of stone that soars 1,700 ft (500 m) above the surrounding plain. Shiprock is all that is left of a 27 million-year-old volcano vent. It can be seen from 100 miles (160 km) away. It is sacred to the Navajo people, and visitors are not allowed to climb it.

Delicate Arch, Arches National Park, Utah

BUILDING WITH ROCK

A walk around a big building, such as a bank or town hall, is like a visit to a rock museum. It's a chance to see how useful rocks are in everyday life.

GRANITE — This rock can be used for the base of the walls because it is very tough. It formed from melted rocks deep in the Earth's crust. Granite forms very slowly, so the crystals within it have time to grow to a large size. They give the rock its speckled look.

LIMESTONE — The columns and steps of entrances are often made with creamy white limestone that's packed with fossil shells. The shells indicate that the rock formed at the bottom of the sea.

MARBLE — Important buildings often have floors of marble because it looks so beautiful when polished. Marble is a kind of metamorphic rock made from limestone that was heated and squeezed deep underground.

GREAT EIGHT

More than 98 percent of all the rocks in the world are formed from a combination of just eight common elements.

ELEMENT	% OF ALL ROCKS
Oxygen	46.5%
Silicon	27.6%
Aluminum	8.0%
Iron	5.0%
Calcium	3.6%
Sodium	2.8%
Potassium	2.6%
Magnesium	2.0%
Total	**98.1%**

CARVING ROCK

Marble is famously beautiful. The great Italian artist Michelangelo Buonarotti (1475–1564) used fine marble from Carrara, Italy, for his sculptures. This rock is extremely white, and so pure and translucent (light filters into the surface a short way) that his statues can appear to be almost human.

Michelangelo's sculpture of David, in Florence, Italy.

SPACE ROCKS

RAINING ROCKS

Meteorites are rocks from the solar system that have bumped into Earth. The biggest meteorites weigh many tons, but most are far smaller. About 20,000 fall from the sky each year.

Name	Where it landed	How big
Hoba meteorite	Namibia, 80,000 years ago	over 58 tons (60 tonnes)
Williamette meteorite	Oregon, 1902	13.7 tons (14 tonnes)
Zagami meteorite	Zagami Rock, Nigeria, 1962	39.8 lbs (18 kg)
Y000593 meteorite	Antarctica, 2000	30.3 lbs (13.7 kg)
Sayh al Uhaymir 008	Oman, 1999	18.8 lbs (8.5 kg)
Shergotty meteorite	Bihar State, India, 1865	11.1 lbs (5 kg)
Nakhla meteorite	El-Nakhla village, Egypt, 1911	11.1 lbs (5 kg)

METEORITE HISTORY

- The oldest meteorites are as old as the solar system – about 4.6 billion years old. Some have traces of the space dust that existed as the planets formed.

- Most meteorites come from asteroids, a few from comets, and some from the Moon and Mars.

- A typical meteorite enters Earth's atmosphere at 6.2–43 miles (10–70 km) per second.

- In 1908, in western Siberia, Russia, a small meteorite exploded on its way to Earth, about 6 miles (10 km) above the ground. The falling sparks and rocks set off forest fires and knocked down every tree within a radius of 20 miles (32 km).

- One Moon meteorite landed at Calcalong Creek in Australia. It was found in 1990 and is the first lunar meteorite found outside Antarctica.

This meteorite formed 1,300 million years ago. It probably came from Mars.

TYPES OF METEORITES

There are three main types of meteorite, each made from different minerals and metals.

- Ninety-three percent of meteorites are stony. They are made of minerals rich in silicon and oxygen (similar to minerals found in the Earth's crust), and come from the surface of asteroids.

- Six percent are mostly made of iron and nickel, and come from the core of big asteroids.

- Stony-iron meteorites contain a mixture of minerals. They come from the inner crust of asteroids that were big enough to have melted inside – therefore mixing the minerals.

MOON ROCK

Aside from meteorites, our only other samples from space are just over 220 lbs (100 kg) of rocks collected from the Moon in the 1960s and 1970s. The most common rock brought back is a type of basalt that is also found on Earth.

The mission badge from Apollo 11, 1969. Astronauts on the mission collected Moon rock samples.

MARS METEORITES

- Most rocks lost from Mars drift into the great unknown, but a few eventually find their way to Earth. We know they come from Mars because they carry traces of the planet's distinctive atmosphere.

- Some 22 Mars meteorites have been found so far.

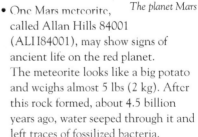

The planet Mars

- One Mars meteorite, called Allan Hills 84001 (ALH84001), may show signs of ancient life on the red planet. The meteorite looks like a big potato and weighs almost 5 lbs (2 kg). After this rock formed, about 4.5 billion years ago, water seeped through it and left traces of fossilized bacteria.

- ALH84001 was chipped off the surface of Mars by an asteroid or comet and began a 16 million-year trip to Earth. It arrived in a meteor shower 13,000 years ago, and was picked up in Antarctica by NASA in 1984.

161

MINERAL FOLKLORE

YOUR OFFICIAL BIRTHSTONE

People once believed that gems came from the sky, and that good luck was gained by wearing the birthstone for their month of birth. People born in June, for example, wore a pearl. Many people still follow this tradition.

MONTH OF THE YEAR	BIRTHSTONE	COLOR OF BIRTHSTONE	
January	Garnet	Dark red	
February	Amethyst	Purple	
March	Aquamarine	Pale blue	
April	Diamond	Transparent white	
May	Emerald	Bright green	
June	Pearl	Cream	
July	Ruby	Red	
August	Peridot	Pale green	
September	Sapphire	Deep blue	
October	Opal	Variegated	
November	Topaz	Yellow	
December	Turquoise	Sky blue	

SPARKLING SUPERSTITIONS

- Some legends state that garnet shines so brightly that Noah used a red garnet to light the Ark.

- The ancient Persians believed that the world rested on a giant sapphire.

- The ancient Greeks believed amethysts could guard against drunkenness.

- The ancient Greek philosopher Plato (427–347 B.C.) believed that all gems were living things – created by a chemical reaction of human spirits.

- The Greek philosopher Theophrastus (371–287 B.C.) divided rubies into male and female – the male rubies had a brighter glow.

- The Romans thought that dedicating emeralds to the goddess Venus would increase their fertility.

- The Spanish conquerors of Mexico believed that jade, if worn close to the side of the body, had the power to cure ailing kidneys.

GEM OF THE DAY

There is a gemstone for each day of the week.

DAY	GEMSTONE
Monday	Pearl
Tuesday	Emerald or ruby
Wednesday	Amethyst
Thursday	Carnelian
Friday	Emerald
Saturday	Diamond
Sunday	Topaz

STRANGE FEELINGS

Some minerals, especially the softer ones, feel very odd when you run your fingers over them.

MINERAL	WHAT IT FEELS LIKE
Copper	Jagged if found as a pure metal
Serpentine	Oily
Talc	Greasy

Copper-encrusted rock

PECULIAR SMELLS

Some minerals have unexpected odors. These are due to the elements that they contain. Usually the smell is not very strong, unless a sample is freshly crushed or broken.

MINERAL	WHAT IT SMELLS LIKE
Arsenopyrite	Garlic
Clay	Dank
Marcasite	Rotting eggs
Sulfur	Rotting eggs (as the sulfur reacts with the air)

Crystals of yellow sulfur

ODD TASTES

Certain minerals have a curious flavor. You can test this if you lick a finger, dab it on the mineral, and taste. (Do not lick the mineral – it may be bad for you.)

MINERAL	WHAT IT TASTES LIKE
Borax	Sweet and slightly stale
Epsomite	Bitter
Glauberite	Salty and bitter
Halite	Salty
Melanterite	Sweet and metallic
Sylvite	Bitter

TREASURE HUNT

STOLEN TREASURE

- The greatest treasure haul ever was that of the Spanish explorer Francisco Pizarro (1475–1541). In 1532, he held the emperor of the Incas, in Peru, to ransom in exchange for one room filled with gold and another filled with silver twice over. The immense value of this loot has never been calculated.

- In 1671, three men tricked their way into the Tower of London. They overwhelmed the guards and made off with the crown, the orb, and the scepter – royal jewels beyond price. The heist ended when the men were captured at the East Gate of the Tower.

- The most successful jewelry robbery of all time, according to *The Guinness Book of Records*, took place in France in 1994. Three men burst into the Carlton Hotel in Cannes, firing machine guns. They ransacked the hotel's jewelry store, just as it was about to close, and ran off with an amazing £30 million of diamonds and other jewels.

GOLD FEVER

- In 1848, in California, a group of men building a sawmill found flakes of gold. This triggered the California Gold Rush, which saw tens of thousands of prospectors pour into the area, all hoping to strike it lucky.

- In 1851, a large amount of gold was found in Victoria, Australia. It set off another frantic gold rush. Within nine years, Australia's population tripled.

- One lucky day in 1886, a man digging stones to build a house struck gold in Witwatersrand. Since then, South Africa has produced more gold than the rest of the world.

Gold prospectors at Ballarat, Australia, in 1851.

PANNING FOR GOLD

The best place to find gold is in streams.

Golddigger panning for gold in Gold Reef City, South Africa

- Gold is 19 times heavier than water, so it sinks to the bottom of a stream and comes to rest in the sand on the stream's bends and banks.
- Gold panners put a few handfuls of gravel and sand into their pan.
- They hold the pan underwater and swirl it with a circular motion. The water carries away the lighter material.
- They lift the pan out of the stream and swirl it with some more water until almost all the gravel has gone.
- The fine sand that's left at the bottom of the pan or on the riffles (little ledges) on the side may have gold in it. Panners use tweezers or a suction pipette to suck up any flecks of gold they can find.

DIAMOND FIND

There are not many places in the world where you can walk around and pick up diamonds. One is the Crater of Diamonds State Park in Arkansas, which sits at the top of an ancient volcanic pipe.

- A diamond was first found here in 1906, when the place was a farm.
- In 1972, it became a state park open to the public.
- It attracts about 74,000 visitors per year.

- The biggest diamond found here weighed 40 carats. Since the time the mine was turned into a park, the record has been 16 carats.
- About 600 diamonds are discovered here every year – that is 70,000 so far.
- The average diamond found is the size of a match head.
- As well as diamonds, people find other gems, including peridots, garnets, agates, and amethysts.
- Any treasure you find is yours to keep.

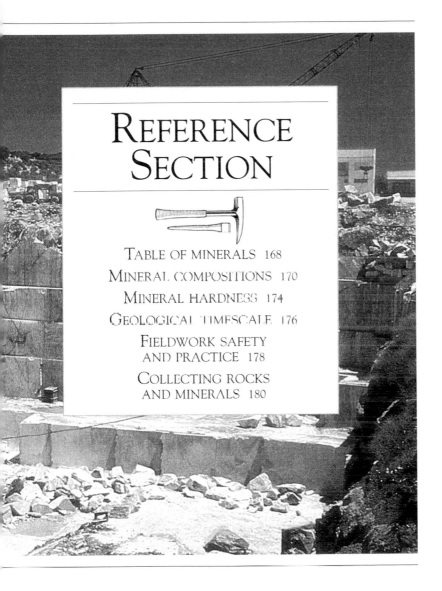

REFERENCE SECTION

TABLE OF MINERALS

THE MINERALS IN THE mineral section of this book are listed below alphabetically. The first column gives a mineral's hardness on Mohs' scale. Its specific gravity (SG) is given in the second column. The last column highlights key features or properties of the mineral.

MINERAL	HARDNESS	SG	COMMENT/PROPERTY
Aegirine	6	3.55–3.6	Pyroxene; relatively rare group member
Albite	6–6.5	2.6–2.63	Feldspar; common rock former
Almandine	7–7.5	4.1–4.3	Gemstone; red garnet variety
Amethyst	7	2.65	Gemstone; purple variety of quartz
Aquamarine	7–8	2.6–2.9	Gemstone; bluish-green variety of beryl
Augite	5.5–6	3.23–3.52	Pyroxene; common rock former
Azurite	3.5–4	3.77–3.78	Produces pigment known as azure blue
Barite	3–3.5	4.5	Crystals feel unusually heavy
Beryl	7–8	2.6–2.9	Gemstone; occurs in many colors
Biotite	2.5–3	2.7–3.4	Mica; usually has a dark color
Calcite	3	2.71	Rock former in limestone and marble
Cassiterite	6–7	7	Tin ore; has crystalline appearance
Chalcedony	7	2.65	Varieties include agate and jasper
Chalcopyrite	3.5–4	4.3–4.4	Fool's gold mineral; copper ore
Chromdravite	7–7.5	3–3.2	Gemstone; green variety of tourmaline
Cinnabar	2–2.5	8–8.2	Main ore of mercury
Citrine	7	2.65	Gemstone; yellow variety of quartz
Copper	2.5–3	8.9	Metallic element; conducts electricity
Corundum	9	4–4.1	Gemstone; extremely hard mineral
Diamond	10	3.52	Hardest naturally occurring mineral
Diopside	5.5–6.5	3.22–3.28	Pyroxene; common rock former
Emerald	7–8	2.6–2.9	Gemstone; green variety of beryl
Enstatite	5–6	3.2–3.4	Pyroxene; common rock former
Fluorite	4	3.18	Occurs in many colors; melts easily
Forsterite	6.5–7	3.27–4.32	Variety of olivine
Galena	2.5	7.58	Ore mineral of lead and silver

MINERAL	HARDNESS	SG	COMMENT/PROPERTY
Glaucophane	6	3.08–3.15	Amphibole; often has violet color
Gold	2.5–3	19.3	Precious metallic element
Graphite	1–2	2.2	Soft mineral made of pure carbon
Grossular	6.5–7	3.4–3.6	Gemstone; lightest-colored garnet
Gypsum	2	2.32	Used in plaster of Paris and alabaster
Halite	2	2.1–2.2	Commonly known as table salt
Heliodor	7–8	2.6–2.9	Gemstone; yellow variety of beryl
Hematite	5–6	5.26	Iron ore; produces ocher pigment
Hornblende	5–6	3.28–3.41	Amphibole; common rock former
Jadeite	6–7	3.24	Pyroxene; commonly known as jade
Labradorite	6–6.5	2.69–2.72	Feldspar; often shows iridescence
Lazurite	5–5.5	2.4–2.5	Main mineral in lapis lazuli
Magnetite	5.5–6.5	5.2	Iron ore; has natural magnetism
Malachite	3.5–4	4	Produces bright green pigment
Marcasite	6–6.5	4.92	Fool's gold mineral; decays in air
Mercury	Liquid	13.6–14.4	Metallic element; can occur as a liquid
Morganite	7–8	2.6–2.9	Gemstone; pink variety of beryl
Muscovite	2.5–4	2.77–2.88	Mica; common rock former
Nephrite	6.5	2.9–3.1	Amphibole; commonly known as jade
Olivine	6.5–7	3.27–4.32	Rock former; gem variety is peridot
Opal	5.5–6.5	1.9–2.3	Gemstone; valued for its rich colors
Platinum	4–4.5	21.4	Precious metallic element
Pyrite	6–6.5	5	Fool's gold mineral
Pyrope	7–7.5	3.5–3.8	Gemstone; purplish-red garnet variety
Quartz	7	2.65	Most common mineral in Earth's crust
Riebeckite	5	3.32–3.38	Amphibole; common rock former
Ruby	9	4–4.1	Gemstone; red variety of corundum
Sapphire	9	4–4.1	Gemstone; blue variety of corundum
Schorl	7–7.5	3–3.2	Black variety of tourmaline
Silver	2.5–3	10.5	Precious metallic element
Sphalerite	3.5–4	3.9–4.1	Main ore of zinc
Sulfur	1.5–2.5	2–2.5	Burns with a blue flame
Sylvite	2	1.99	Bitter-tasting rock salt
Tourmaline	7–7.5	3–3.2	Gemstone; occurs in many colors
Tremolite	5–6	2.9–3.2	Amphibole; can be mined for asbestos
Turquoise	5–6	2.6–2.8	Gemstone; excellent carving material

TABLE OF MINERALS

MINERAL COMPOSITIONS

THE COMPOSITION OF A mineral gives it properties, such as color and hardness. Some minerals consist of a single element. An example is diamond, which contains only carbon. Most minerals, however, are compounds or mixtures of elements. For example, quartz is a compound of silicon and oxygen.

Table of elements

The full table of elements is given below. The scientific symbols for the elements are in the left column. Their full names are given in the right column. The table lists the symbols in alphabetical order. Some of these elements appear in the list of mineral formulas on pages 172–3.

SYMBOL	NAME	SYMBOL	NAME	SYMBOL	NAME
Ac	Actinium	Bi	Bismuth	Cr	Chromium
Ag	Silver	Bk	Berkelium	Cs	Cesium
Al	Aluminum	Br	Bromine	Cu	Copper
Am	Americium	C	Carbon	Dy	Dysprosium
Ar	Argon	Ca	Calcium	Er	Erbium
As	Arsenic	Cd	Cadmium	Es	Einsteinium
At	Astatine	Ce	Cerium	Eu	Europium
Au	Gold	Cf	Californium	F	Fluorine
B	Boron	Cl	Chlorine	Fe	Iron
Ba	Barium	Cm	Curium	Fm	Fermium
Be	Beryllium	Co	Cobalt	Fr	Francium

Symbol	Name
Ga	Gallium
Gd	Gadolinium
Ge	Germanium
H	Hydrogen
He	Helium
Hf	Hafnium
Hg	Mercury
Ho	Holmium
I	Iodine
In	Indium
Ir	Iridium
K	Potassium
Kr	Krypton
La	Lanthanum
Li	Lithium
Lr	Lawrencium
Lu	Lutetium
Md	Mendelevium
Mg	Magnesium
Mn	Manganese
Mo	Molybdenum
N	Nitrogen
Na	Sodium
Nb	Niobium
Nd	Neodymium
Ne	Neon

Symbol	Name
Ni	Nickel
No	Nobelium
Np	Neptunium
O	Oxygen
Os	Osmium
P	Phosphorus
Pa	Protactinium
Pb	Lead
Pd	Palladium
Pm	Promethium
Po	Polonium
Pr	Praseodymium
Pt	Platinum
Pu	Plutonium
Ra	Radium
Rb	Rubidium
Re	Rhenium
Rh	Rhodium
Rn	Radon
Ru	Ruthenium
S	Sulfur
Sb	Antimony
Sc	Scandium
Se	Selenium
Si	Silicon
Sm	Samarium

Symbol	Name
Sn	Tin
Sr	Strontium
Ta	Tantalum
Tb	Terbium
Tc	Technetium
Te	Tellurium
Th	Thorium
Ti	Titanium
Tl	Thallium
Tm	Thulium
U	Uranium
Une	Unnilennium
Unh	Unnilhexium
Uno	Unniloctium
Unp	Unnilpentium
Unq	Unnilquadium
Uns	Unnilseptium
V	Vanadium
W	Tungsten
Xe	Xenon
Y	Yttrium
Yb	Ytterbium
Zn	Zinc
Zr	Zirconium

MINERAL COMPOSITIONS

Mineral formulas

The compositions of the minerals in the mineral section of this book appear below as formulas. A formula shows how different atoms make up a mineral. For example, halite (NaCl) is made up of sodium (Na) and chlorine (Cl) atoms.

Note: A subscripted number ($_2$) shows how many atoms of one element are joined to atoms of another element. For example, two oxygen atoms (O_2) are joined to one atom of silicon (Si) in quartz (SiO_2).

MINERAL	CHEMICAL FORMULA
Aegirine	$NaFeSi_2O_6$
Albite	$NaAlSi_3O_8$
Almandine	$Fe_3Al_2(SiO_4)_3$
Amethyst	SiO_2
Aquamarine	$Be_3Al_2Si_6O_{18}$
Augite	$CaNa(Mg,Fe,Al)(Al, Si)_2O_6$
Azurite	$Cu_3(CO_3)_2(OH)_2$
Barite	$BaSO_4$
Beryl	$Be_3Al_2Si_6O_{18}$
Biotite	$K(Mg,Fe)_3(Al,Fe)Si_3O_{10}(OH,F)_2$
Calcite	$CaCO_3$
Cassiterite	SnO_2
Chalcedony	SiO_2
Chalcopyrite	$CuFeS_2$
Chromdravite	$Na(Mg,Fe,Al,Mn,Li)_3Al_6(BO_3)_3(Si_6O_{18})(OH,F)_4$
Cinnabar	HgS
Copper	Cu
Corundum	Al_2O_3
Diamond	C
Diopside	$CaMgSi_2O_6$
Emerald	$Be_3Al_2Si_6O_{18}$
Enstatite	$MgSiO_3$
Fluorite	CaF_2
Forsterite	Mg_2SiO_4
Galena	PbS
Glaucophane	$Na_2(Mg,Fe)_3Al_2Si_8O_{22}(OH)_2$

Mineral	Chemical formula
Gold	Au
Graphite	C
Grossular	$Ca_3Al_2(SiO_4)_3$
Gypsum	$CaSO_42H_2O$
Halite	$NaCl$
Heliodor	$Be_3Al_2Si_6O_{18}$
Hematite	Fe_2O_3
Hornblende	$NaCa_2(Mg,Fe,Al)_5(Si,Al)_8O_{22}(OH)_2$
Jadeite	$NaAlSi_2O_6$
Labradorite	$(Na,Ca)Al_{1-2}Si_{3-2}O_8$
Lazurite	$(Na,Ca)_8(Al,Si)_{12}O_{24}(S,SO)_4$
Magnetite	Fe_3O_4
Malachite	$Cu_2CO_3(OH)_2$
Marcasite	FeS_2
Mercury	Hg
Morganite	$Be_3Al_2Si_6O_{18}$
Muscovite	$KAl_3Si_3O_{10}(OH)_2$
Nephrite	$Ca_2(Mg,Fe)_5Si_8O_{22}(OH)_2$
Olivine	Mg_2SiO_4
Opal	SiO_2nH_2O
Platinum	Pt
Pyrite	FeS_2
Pyrope	$Mg_3Al_2(SiO_4)_3$
Quartz	SiO_2
Riebeckite	$Na_2Fe_3Fe_2Si_8O_{22}(OH)_2$
Ruby	Al_2O_3
Sapphire	Al_2O_3
Schorl	$Na(Mg,Fe,Al,Mn,Li)_3Al_6(BO_3)_3(Si_6O_{18})(OH,F)_4$
Silver	Ag
Sphalerite	ZnS
Sulfur	S
Sylvite	KCl
Tourmaline	$Na(Mg,Fe,Al,Mn,Li)_3Al_6(BO_3)_3(Si_6O_{18})(OH,F)_4$
Tremolite	$Ca_2Mg_5Si_8O_{22}(OH)_2$
Turquoise	$CuAl_6(PO_4)_4(OH)_84H_2O$

MINERAL HARDNESS

SCRATCHING IS AN EASY way to gauge mineral hardness. In 1812, the Austrian mineralogist Friedrich Mohs (1773–1839) set a scale of mineral hardness from talc (1) to diamond (10) that is still used today. Any mineral on the scale will only scratch those minerals below it.

FRIEDRICH MOHS

---

1 TALC

HARDNESS
Talc is one of the softest minerals. It is useful as a powder and is the main ingredient in talcum powder.

TESTING
Minerals with a Mohs' hardness of 1 feel greasy and can be scratched with a fingernail.

---

2 GYPSUM

HARDNESS
Gypsum is formed when sea water evaporates at the Earth's surface. Surface-forming minerals are usually soft.

TESTING
Fingernails contain a tough protein that can scratch minerals with a hardness of 2.

---

3 CALCITE

HARDNESS
Limestones and most shells contain calcite. Animals take the calcite they need to make their shells from seawater.

TESTING
A copper coin will scratch minerals of hardness 3. The coin must be real copper.

---

4 FLUORITE

HARDNESS
Fluorite is a good decorative mineral. It is soft enough to carve, but hard enough to keep a good polish.

TESTING
Hardness 4 minerals are easy to scratch with window glass, which is made from quartz sand.

---

5 APATITE

HARDNESS
Human and animal bones are made from forms of apatite. It is a hard material that usually bends rather than breaks.

TESTING
Window glass will scratch minerals that have a hardness of between 5 and 6.

6 ORTHOCLASE

HARDNESS
Orthoclase is a type of feldspar. The gem variety of this mineral, moonstone, is one of the harder gemstones.

TESTING
A sharp piece of steel, such as a file, scratches minerals with a hardness of up to 6.5.

7 QUARTZ

HARDNESS
The most valuable gemstones are harder than quartz because they resist scratching by this common mineral.

TESTING
Quartz is too hard to scratch with everyday materials, but it can test softer substances.

8 TOPAZ

HARDNESS
Gem topaz is rare, but can form large crystals. Although it is hard, topaz breaks easily along a single cleavage plane.

TESTING
Minerals of hardness 8 and above are very rare, so scratch tests are not usually needed.

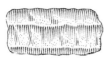

9 CORUNDUM

HARDNESS
This mineral has two valuable gem varieties, sapphire and ruby. Both are prized for their color and extreme hardness.

TESTING
Corundum leaves a mark on most other minerals on the scale, except diamond.

10 DIAMOND

HARDNESS
Diamond is the hardest mineral. It is many times harder than corundum, which is just below it on Mohs' scale.

TESTING
The only natural substance that can scratch a diamond is another diamond.

GEOLOGICAL TIMESCALE

BY STUDYING ROCKS and fossils, geologists have built up a history of the Earth. It is divided into periods, which are shown in this spiral diagram. Our planet formed about 4,600 million years ago (MYA) in the Pre-Cambrian period. Many changes have occurred since – changes that are recorded in the rocks and fossils of today.

CRETACEOUS (144–65 MYA)
The dinosaurs, including three-horned *Triceratops*, become extinct.

CAMBRIAN (550–510 MYA)
Animals with shells develop, such as this trilobite, *Xystridura*.

ORDOVICIAN (510–438 MYA)
The first fishes appear in shallow seas.

DEVONIAN (408–362 MYA)
The seas fill with bony fish like this *Pterichthyodes*.

SILURIAN (438–408 MYA)
Oxygen-forming plants appear on land.

PRE-CAMBRIAN (4,600–550 MYA)
Simple plants and animals evolve.

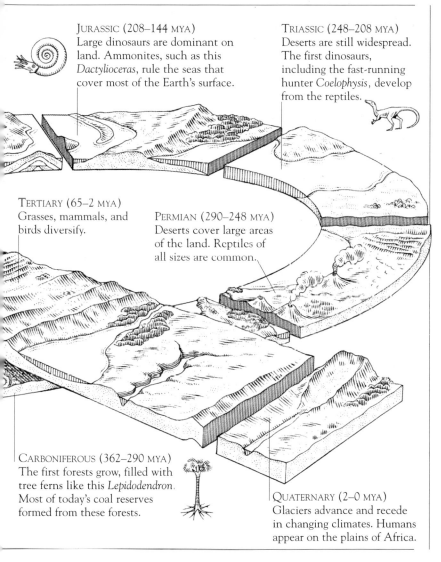

JURASSIC (208–144 MYA)
Large dinosaurs are dominant on land. Ammonites, such as this *Dactylioceras*, rule the seas that cover most of the Earth's surface.

TRIASSIC (248–208 MYA)
Deserts are still widespread. The first dinosaurs, including the fast-running hunter *Coelophysis*, develop from the reptiles.

TERTIARY (65–2 MYA)
Grasses, mammals, and birds diversify.

PERMIAN (290–248 MYA)
Deserts cover large areas of the land. Reptiles of all sizes are common.

CARBONIFEROUS (362–290 MYA)
The first forests grow, filled with tree ferns like this *Lepidodendron*. Most of today's coal reserves formed from these forests.

QUATERNARY (2–0 MYA)
Glaciers advance and recede in changing climates. Humans appear on the plains of Africa.

FIELDWORK SAFETY AND PRACTICE

FIELDWORK IS PART of the enjoyment of collecting rocks and minerals. Your search for good specimens may take you to interesting places both in your locality and farther afield. On a collecting trip, treat your chosen site with respect so that it can be enjoyed by others. You should also be aware of safety. These pages contain some simple tips for new collectors. It is also a good idea to seek the advice of experienced collectors or the national societies.

FIELDWORK CODE

• Take only photographs and leave only your footprints.

• Do not go collecting alone. Join a local group.

• Make sure you take proper safety equipment on a collecting trip.

• Before setting out on a field trip, find out as much as possible about the intended collecting site.

• Always seek permission in advance for fieldwork on private land.

• Be careful not to disturb or harm wildlife around the collecting site.

• Think about other collectors and leave sites tidy and safe.

• Do not leave behind or drop broken rock fragments – they may harm people and wildlife.

• Coastal sites, disused and working quarries, and cliff faces may be very dangerous for fieldwork. Avoid collecting from these sites unless you are under expert supervision.

• Always tell other people where you intend to go on a field trip, especially when collecting in potentially dangerous and remote areas like hills or mountains.

SAFETY ON SITE

Experienced rock and mineral collectors are very aware of safety. These are the typical things they take with them on every field trip.

- Protective clothing – warm, waterproof clothes and good walking boots are essential.
- Safety equipment, including a hard hat, shatterproof goggles, and protective gloves. These must be worn at all times during fieldwork, particularly during hammering.
- A first-aid kit.
- Something to eat and drink.

EQUIPMENT FOR RECORDING SAMPLES IN THE FIELD

CAMERA

SKETCHPAD AND PENCIL

PHOTOGRAPHIC FILM

SAFETY EQUIPMENT

STRONG GLOVES

HARD HAT

FIRST-AID KIT

PROTECTIVE GOGGLES

OTHER POINTS TO REMEMBER

- It is often better to observe and record samples with a camera or sketchpad than remove them from a site. This leaves a site undamaged by hammering and preserves the sample.
- Only collect specimens when absolutely necessary and remove as few specimens as possible.
- Never collect from buildings, bridges, or walls.
- Don't tamper with machinery.

IDENTIFYING A SPECIMEN

This simple kit may help you identify a specimen on site. After a close look with a hand lens, the penknife and coins will test the specimen's hardness.

PENKNIFE

COINS

HAND LENS

COLLECTING ROCKS AND MINERALS

PLAN A COLLECTING trip in advance. It is a good idea to research the site and the type of specimens you expect to find there. Good sites have abundant samples that can be collected safely and without harming the landscape. They are usually well known – ask at your local museum, library, or university.

COLLECTORS' EQUIPMENT

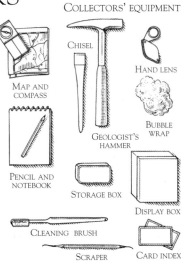

MAP AND COMPASS

CHISEL

HAND LENS

GEOLOGIST'S HAMMER

BUBBLE WRAP

PENCIL AND NOTEBOOK

STORAGE BOX

DISPLAY BOX

CLEANING BRUSH

SCRAPER

CARD INDEX

Hard hat

Map and compass

FINDING AND IDENTIFYING A SITE
You may need to use a map and compass to locate your collecting site. An ordinary map contains other useful information, such as the location of nearby cliffs and beaches. Detailed geological maps showing the position and age of rock structures are also available from specialist shops.

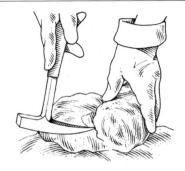

1 RECORDING A SAMPLE
When you find a good sample, make a detailed sketch of its location. Photographs are also useful. Note the map reference of the site in case you want to collect there again. Make sure that you record different samples separately.

2 REMOVING AND PACKING
If you do take a sample home, chip it out and trim it to size with a hammer. Don't forget to wear protective gloves and goggles. Wrap each sample using bubble wrap, newspaper, or tissue – this prevents scratching on the journey home.

3 CLEANING AND IDENTIFICATION
At home, unpack and clean your samples. Be careful if you wash them in water – you don't want your samples to dissolve. You may need a hand lens for identification.

4 INDEXING AND STORING
When you have identified your rock or mineral, store it carefully. Each specimen needs a label giving its name and original site. An index may be useful for larger collections.

Glossary

ALLOY
A mixture of two types of metal, or a metal and a nonmetal.

ATOM
Smallest part of an element that can exist.

BIOGENIC SEDIMENTARY ROCK
Rock that forms from the fossilized remains of plants and animals.

BOTRYOIDAL HABIT
Rounded, bubbly habit.

CARAT
The standard measure of weight for precious stones and metals. One carat is equivalent to 0.006 oz (0.2 g).

CHATOYANCY
Silky appearance on surface of a mineral. It is also known as the "cat's eye" effect.

CHEMICAL SEDIMENTARY ROCK
Rock that is formed by mineral precipitation.

CLASTS
Fragments in sedimentary rocks that originally formed part of other rocks.

CLEAVAGE
The way a mineral breaks along planes according to its atomic structure.

COMPOUND
Material made up of more than one element.

CONTACT METAMORPHIC ROCK
Rock that forms as the heat from magma or a lava flow alters an existing rock.

CORE
Region of iron and nickel that makes up the center of the Earth. It is about 850 miles (1,370 km) across.

COUNTRY ROCK
Existing rock that is altered by igneous or metamorphic processes.

CRUST
The thin outer layer of the Earth. It is between 4⅓ and 43½ miles (7 and 70 km) thick.

CRYSTAL SYSTEMS
The systems into which crystals are grouped according to symmetry. There are six main crystal systems: cubic, monoclinic, triclinic, trigonal/hexagonal, orthorhombic, and tetragonal.

DENDRITIC HABIT
Branching, or treelike habit.

DETRITAL SEDIMENTARY ROCK
Rock that is made up of broken fragments of other rocks.

DIAPIR
Large dome of salt, usually beneath the Earth's surface. These structures often trap reserves of oil and gas.

DOUBLE REFRACTION
An optical effect in which an object appears double when viewed through a transparent crystal.

DYKE
Sheet of igneous rock that breaks across existing rock structures.

ELEMENT
Material that cannot be broken down into more simple substances by chemical means.

EROSION
The transportation of material from its original site by processes involving wind, water, and ice.

EVAPORITE
Material left behind when water evaporates.

EXTRUSIVE IGNEOUS ROCK
Igneous rock that forms at the Earth's surface.

FACET
One side of a cut gemstone.

FIBROUS HABIT
Fiberlike habit.

FLUORESCENCE
Optical effect whereby a mineral appears a different color in ultraviolet light than in ordinary daylight.

FOLIATIONS
Patterns caused by aligned crystals in metamorphic rocks.

GALVANIZATION
The process of adding zinc to other metals or alloys to prevent corrosion and rust.

GEMSTONE
A mineral, usually crystalline, that derives particular value from its color, rarity, and hardness.

GEOLOGIST
A person who studies the Earth.

GRANULAR HABIT
Grainlike habit.

HABIT
The general appearance or shape of a mineral.

HOPPER CRYSTAL
Crystal with regular, stepped depressions on each face.

HYDROTHERMAL VEIN
A crack or fracture in a rock filled with hot, water-rich solutions that flow from underground igneous masses.

IDIOCHROMATIC MINERAL
Mineral that is almost always the same color because of certain light-absorbing atoms that form an essential part of its makeup.

IGNEOUS ROCK
Rock formed as magma cools and hardens in the Earth's crust.

INCLUSION
Crystals of one mineral that are enclosed in crystals of another mineral.

INTRUSIVE IGNEOUS ROCK
Igneous rock that forms beneath the Earth's surface.

IRIDESCENCE
A play of colors on the surface of a mineral like a film of oil on water.

LAVA
Magma at the Earth's surface.

LUSTER
The way a mineral shines. It is affected by light reflecting off the surface of the mineral.

MAGMA
Molten rock beneath the Earth's surface.

MAGMA CHAMBER
Underground reservoir of magma that feeds a volcano. It can harden to form a pluton.

MANTLE
Layer of the Earth between the core and the crust. It is approximately 1,800 miles (2,900 km) thick.

MASSIVE HABIT
Mineral habit that has no definite shape.

MATRIX
Mass of rock in which crystals are set.

METAMORPHIC ROCK
Rock that forms due to the action of heat and pressure, or heat alone.

METAMORPHISM
The action of heat and pressure.

METEORITE
Object from outer space that survives the passage through the atmosphere to reach Earth.

MINERAL
A solid mixture of chemicals that has certain regular characteristics, such as atomic structure and chemical composition.

MINERAL LODE
Vein of metal ore.

MINERAL VEIN
Cracks in rocks that become filled with hot, mineral-rich liquids.

MOHS' SCALE
Scale devised by the Austrian mineralogist Friedrich Mohs that measures the hardness of minerals by scratching.

NATIVE ELEMENT
Element that occurs naturally in a free state. In other words, it does not form part of a compound.

OOLITH
Small, rounded grains that make up some sedimentary rocks.

OPAQUE MATERIAL
Material that does not allow light to pass through it.

ORE
Rock or other material from which a metal is extracted.

ORGANIC SEDIMENTARY ROCK
Rock that is made up of the remains of plants and trees.

PEGMATITE
Igneous rock that consists of unusually large crystals.

PERFECT CLEAVAGE
Property of a mineral that breaks only in certain directions.

PIEZOELECTRICITY
Generation of positive and negative charges across a crystal that has pressure applied to it.

PIGMENT
A natural coloring material often used in paints and dyes.

PLATE
Large "panels" that form the Earth's surface.

PLEOCHROISM
Optical property of a mineral where the color of a crystal changes if the crystal is viewed from a different angle.

PLUTON
Large mass of igneous rock that forms beneath the Earth's surface as magma solidifies.

PRECIPITATION
Chemical process whereby a solid substance is deposited from solution in a liquid.

PRISMATIC CRYSTAL
Crystal that is longer in one direction than the other.

RADIOMETRIC DATING
A precise method of dating rocks that measures the rate of decay of radioactive atoms in a rock.

REGIONAL METAMORPHIC ROCK
Rock that forms from the action of heat and pressure on existing rocks, usually in mountain-building areas.

RENIFORM HABIT
Habit that resembles an animal kidney.

Rock
Solid mixtures, or aggregates, of minerals.

Secondary ore
A mineral or rock that develops from the remains of other ore minerals and thereby becomes an ore itself.

Sedimentary rock
Rock that forms at the Earth's surface. It consists of layers of rock fragments or other substances that have been deposited on top of each other.

Sill
Sheet of igneous rock that follows existing rock structures.

Specific gravity
The comparison of a mineral's weight with the weight of an equal volume of water.

Streak
The color of a mineral's powder. It is often a more useful identification tool than color because it gives less variable results.

Striations
Parallel lines on a crystal face that develop as the crystal grows.

Structural metamorphic rock
Rock that forms in extreme pressure caused by movements in the Earth's crust.

Tarnishing
Chemical reaction that occurs on the surface of a mineral that alters the mineral's characteristic color or luster.

Thermal metamorphic rock
Rock that is altered by the action of heat alone.

Tor
Granite landform characterized by large blocks of rock separated by cracks. The rock originally formed underground, becoming exposed as weathering and erosion removed surrounding rocks.

Translucent material
Material that allows daylight to pass through it. Objects cannot be seen clearly through a translucent material.

Transparent material
Material that allows daylight to pass through

it. Objects can be seen clearly through a transparent mineral.

Twinned crystals
Two or more crystals of the same mineral that intersect each other along a common, or shared, plane.

Vesicle
A rounded cavity in extrusive igneous rocks that is left by a gas bubble as the rock hardens.

Volcanic bomb
Blob of lava thrown out of a volcano. It solidifies before hitting the ground.

Volcanic vent
Central passage in a volcano through which magma flows and erupts as lava.

Vulcanization
The process of adding sulfur to rubber products to make them stronger and more durable.

Weathering
The breaking down of rocks by the action of various processes such as freezing and thawing and dissolving in water.

INDEX

INDEX

Acknowledgments

Dorling Kindersley would like to thank:
Hilary Bird for the index; Sarah Goulding
for editorial assistance; Joanne Little for
design assistance; Chris Pellant for
consulting on additional material.

Photographs by:
Michael Crockett, Geoff Dann,
Andreas von Einsiedel, Steve Gorton,
Chas Howson, Colin Keates, Dave King,
James Stevenson, Harry Taylor.

Illustrations by:
John Woodcock, Dan Wright.

**Picture credits: t = top b = bottom
c = center l = left r = right**
Archiv fur Kunst/ Museo di Argenti,
Florence 92 bl. Bergakademie Freiberg
174tr. Christie's Images 43cb. Stephanie
Colasanti 129tr. Archive P. et M. Curie
44bc. The Environmental Picture Library/
Graham Burns 11br. ffotograff /Patricia
Aithie 129br. Robert Harding Picture
Library 65 tr; 75tl; 109bl; 117 br/
Ian Griffiths 105tl;/Tomlinson 39c;
Adam Woolfitt 90bl; 126tl. Michael
Holford 53bl; 87tl;91tr. Geoscience
Features 80br. Image Bank/Jeff Bartel
119tr;/Jackie Gucia 126bl;/Johnson
166-167. Impact /Mike Mc Queen
105br;/Tony Page 121 bc;/David Palmer 106
tr/Homer Sykes 89tl;130bl. Johnson Mathey
57tl. Mansell Collection 15cr; 51tr; 73 cl.
Biblioteca Medicea Laurenziana, Florence
63tr. NASA 112bl; 113c; 113br, National
Nuclear Corporation 58bl. Royal Museum
of Scotland /Michel Zabé 55br.
Science Photo Library/Jim Amos 98bl;/Alex
Bartel 119tr;/Jack Fields 71 tl;/David Leah
55tr; /Peter Manzel 48 bc; /N.A.S.A.
14bl;/Soames Summerhays 111tr. Still
Pictures /Roger Stenberg 94 br. Tony
Stone/John Freeman 111bl/ Jacky Gucin
126bl. Wallace Collection 47b.